NARRATIVE OF

FREDERICK DOUGLASS

WITH SELECTED SPEECHES

FREDERICK DOUGLASS

With compelling narratives that have intrigued and inspired generations, the Dover Bookshelf brings classic literature into the twenty-first century with bold new designs that will elicit awe and admiration. These gorgeous editions provide a comfortable reading experience and offer an excellent introduction to the works of beloved authors worldwide, in fiction and nonfiction. The Dover Bookshelf offers the perfect keepsakes to beautify your home or gift to literature lovers.

NARRATIVE OF THE LIFE OF
FREDERICK DOUGLASS

WITH SELECTED SPEECHES

FREDERICK DOUGLASS

DOVER PUBLICATIONS
Garden City, New York

This Dover edition, first published in 2024, is an unabridged, slightly corrected republication of the work first published as *Narrative of the Life of Frederick Douglass, an American Slave* by The Anti-Slavery Office, Boston, in 1845. This edition includes five speeches by Frederick Douglass, accompanied by Editor's Notes by James Daley, which originally appeared in *Great Speeches by Frederick Douglass*, first published by Dover in 2013. Readers should be forewarned that the text contains racial and cultural references of the era in which it was written and may be deemed offensive by today's standards.

ISBN-13: 978-0-486-85330-7
ISBN-10: 0-486-85330-6

Publisher: Betina Cochran
Associate Publisher: Peter Lenz
Managing Editorial Supervisor: Susan Rattiner
Senior Production Editor: Michael Croland
Cover Designer: Peter Donahue
Creative Manager: Marie Zaczkiewicz
Production: Pam Weston, Tammi McKenna, Ayse Yilmaz

Cover and endpaper art: 1897 engraving, artist unknown, GettyImages.com

Manufactured in the United States of America
85330601   2024
www.doverpublications.com

Contents

Narrative of the Life of Frederick Douglass

Preface

In the month of August, 1841, I attended an anti-slavery convention in Nantucket, at which it was my happiness to become acquainted with Frederick Douglass, the writer of the following Narrative. He was a stranger to nearly every member of that body; but, having recently made his escape from the southern prison-house of bondage, and feeling his curiosity excited to ascertain the principles and measures of the abolitionists,—of whom he had heard a somewhat vague description while he was a slave,—he was induced to give his attendance, on the occasion alluded to, though at that time a resident in New Bedford.

Fortunate, most fortunate occurrence!—fortunate for the millions of his manacled brethren, yet panting for deliverance from their awful thraldom!—fortunate for the cause of negro emancipation, and of universal liberty!—fortunate for the land of his birth, which he has already done so much to save and bless!—fortunate for a large circle of friends and acquaintances, whose sympathy and affection he has strongly secured by the many sufferings he has endured, by his virtuous traits of character, by his ever-abiding remembrance of those who are in bonds, as being bound with them!—fortunate for the multitudes, in various parts of our republic, whose minds he has enlightened on the subject of slavery, and who have been melted to tears by his pathos, or roused to virtuous indignation by his stirring eloquence against the enslavers of men!—fortunate for himself, as it at once brought him into the field of public usefulness, "gave the world assurance of a man," quickened the slumbering energies of his soul, and consecrated him to the great work of breaking the rod of the oppressor, and letting the oppressed go free!

I shall never forget his first speech at the convention—the extraordinary emotion it excited in my own mind—the powerful impression it created upon a crowded auditory, completely taken by surprise—the applause which followed from the beginning to the end of his felicitous remarks. I think I never hated slavery so intensely as at that moment; certainly, my perception of the enormous outrage which is inflicted by it, on the godlike nature of its victims, was rendered far more clear than ever. There stood one, in physical proportion and stature commanding and exact— in intellect richly endowed—in natural eloquence a prodigy—in soul manifestly "created but a little lower than the angels"—yet a slave, ay, a fugitive slave,—trembling for his safety, hardly daring to believe that on the American soil, a single white person could be found who would befriend him at all hazards, for the love of God and humanity! Capable of high attainments as an intellectual and moral being—needing nothing but a comparatively small amount of cultivation to make him an ornament to society and a blessing to his race—by the law of the land, by the voice of the people, by the terms of the slave code, he was only a piece of property, a beast of burden, a chattel personal, nevertheless!

A beloved friend from New Bedford prevailed on Mr. DOUGLASS to address the convention. He came forward to the platform with a hesitancy and embarrassment, necessarily the attendants of a sensitive mind in such a novel position. After apologizing for his ignorance, and reminding the audience that slavery was a poor school for the human intellect and heart, he proceeded to narrate some of the facts in his own history as a slave, and in the course of his speech gave utterance to many noble thoughts and thrilling reflections. As soon as he had taken his seat, filled with hope and admiration, I rose, and declared that PATRICK HENRY, of revolutionary fame, never made a speech more eloquent in the cause of liberty, than the one we had just listened to from the lips of that hunted fugitive. So I believed at that time—such is my belief now. I reminded the audience of the peril which surrounded this self-emancipated young man at the North,—even in Massachusetts, on the soil of the Pilgrim Fathers, among the descendants of revolutionary sires; and I appealed to them, whether they would ever allow him to be carried back into slavery,—law or no law, constitution or no constitution. The response was unanimous and in thunder-tones— "NO!" "Will you succor and protect him as a brother-man—a resident of the old Bay State?" "YES!" shouted the whole mass, with an energy so startling, that the ruthless tyrants south of Mason and Dixon's line might almost have heard the mighty burst of feeling, and recognized it as the pledge of an invincible determination, on the part of those who gave it, never to betray him that wanders, but to hide the outcast, and firmly to abide the consequences.

It was at once deeply impressed upon my mind, that, if Mr. DOUGLASS could be persuaded to consecrate his time and talents to the promotion of the anti-slavery enterprise, a powerful impetus would be given to it, and a stunning blow at the same time inflicted on northern prejudice against a colored complexion. I therefore endeavored to instil hope and courage into his mind, in order that he might dare to engage in a vocation so anomalous and responsible for a person in his situation; and I was seconded in this effort by warm-hearted friends, especially by the late General Agent of the Massachusetts Anti-Slavery Society, Mr. JOHN A. COLLINS, whose judgment in this instance entirely coincided with my own. At first, he could give no encouragement; with unfeigned diffidence, he expressed his conviction that he was not adequate to the performance of so great a task; the path marked out was wholly an untrodden one; he was sincerely apprehensive that he should do more harm than good. After much deliberation, however, he consented to make a trial; and ever since that period, he has acted as a lecturing agent, under the auspices either of the American or the Massachusetts Anti-Slavery Society. In labors he has been most abundant; and his success in combating prejudice, in gaining proselytes, in agitating the public mind, has far surpassed the most sanguine expectations that were raised at the commencement of his brilliant career. He has borne himself with gentleness and meekness, yet with true manliness of character. As a public speaker, he excels in pathos, wit, comparison, imitation, strength of reasoning, and fluency of language. There is in him that union of head and heart, which is indispensable to an enlightenment of the heads and a winning of the hearts of others. May his strength continue to be equal to his day! May he continue to "grow in grace, and in the knowledge of God," that he may be increasingly serviceable in the cause of bleeding humanity, whether at home or abroad!

It is certainly a very remarkable fact, that one of the most efficient advocates of the slave population, now before the public, is a fugitive slave, in the person of FREDERICK DOUGLASS; and that the free colored population of the United States are as ably represented by one of their own number, in the person of CHARLES LENOX REMOND, whose eloquent appeals have extorted the highest applause of multitudes on both sides of the Atlantic. Let the calumniators of the colored race despise themselves for their baseness and illiberality of spirit, and henceforth cease to talk of the natural inferiority of those who require nothing but time and opportunity to attain to the highest point of human excellence.

It may, perhaps, be fairly questioned, whether any other portion of the population of the earth could have endured the privations, sufferings and horrors of slavery, without having become more degraded in the scale of humanity than the slaves of African descent. Nothing has been left undone to cripple their intellects, darken their minds, debase their moral nature, obliterate all traces of their relationship to mankind; and yet how wonderfully they have sustained the mighty load of a most frightful bondage, under which they have been groaning for centuries! To illustrate the effect of slavery on the white man,—to show that he has no powers of endurance, in such a condition, superior to those of his black brother,—DANIEL O'CONNELL, the distinguished advocate of universal emancipation, and the mightiest champion of prostrate but not conquered Ireland, relates the following anecdote in a speech delivered by him in the Conciliation Hall, Dublin, before the Loyal National Repeal Association, March 31, 1845. "No matter," said Mr. O'CONNELL, "under what specious term it may disguise itself, slavery is still hideous. *It has a natural, an inevitable tendency to brutalize every noble faculty of man.* An American sailor, who was cast away on the shore of Africa, where he was kept in slavery for three years, was, at the expiration of that period, found to be imbruted and stultified—he had lost all reasoning power; and having forgotten his native language, could only utter some savage gibberish between Arabic and English, which nobody could understand, and which even he himself found difficulty in pronouncing. So much for the humanizing influence of THE DOMESTIC INSTITUTION!" Admitting this to have been an extraordinary case of mental deterioration, it proves at least that the white slave can sink as low in the scale of humanity as the black one.

Mr. DOUGLASS has very properly chosen to write his own Narrative, in his own style, and according to the best of his ability, rather than to employ some one else. It is, therefore, entirely his own production; and, considering how long and dark was the career he had to run as a slave,—how few have been his opportunities to improve his mind since he broke his iron fetters,—it is, in my judgment, highly creditable to his head and heart. He who can peruse it without a tearful eye, a heaving breast, an afflicted spirit,—without being filled with an unutterable abhorrence of slavery and all its abettors, and animated with a determination to seek the immediate overthrow of that execrable system,—without trembling for the fate of this country in the hands of a righteous God, who is ever on the side of the oppressed, and whose arm is not shortened that it cannot save,—must have a flinty heart, and be qualified to act the part of a trafficker "in slaves and the souls of men." I am confident that it is essentially true in all its statements; that nothing has been set down in malice, nothing exaggerated, nothing drawn from the imagination; that it comes short of the reality, rather than overstates a single fact in regard to SLAVERY AS IT IS. The experience of FREDERICK DOUGLASS, as a slave, was not a peculiar one; his lot was not especially a hard one; his case may be regarded as a very fair specimen of the treatment of slaves in Maryland, in which State it is conceded that they are better fed and less cruelly treated than in Georgia, Alabama, or Louisiana. Many have suffered incomparably more, while very few on the plantations have suffered less, than himself. Yet how deplorable was his situation! what terrible chastisements were inflicted upon his person! what still more shocking outrages were perpetrated upon his mind! with all his noble powers and sublime aspirations, how like a brute was he treated, even by those professing to have the same mind in them that was in Christ Jesus! to what dreadful liabilities was he continually subjected! how destitute of friendly counsel and aid, even in his greatest extremities! how heavy was the midnight of woe which shrouded in blackness the last ray of hope, and filled the future with terror and gloom! what longings after freedom took possession of his breast, and how his misery augmented, in proportion as he grew reflective and intelligent,—thus demonstrating that a happy slave is an extinct man! how he thought, reasoned, felt, under the lash of the driver, with the chains upon his limbs! what perils he encountered in his endeavors to escape from his horrible doom! and how signal have been his deliverance and preservation in the midst of a nation of pitiless enemies!

This Narrative contains many affecting incidents, many passages of great eloquence and power; but I think the most thrilling one of them all is the description DOUGLASS gives of his feelings, as he stood soliloquizing respecting his fate, and the chances of his one day being a freeman, on the banks of the Chesapeake Bay—viewing the receding vessels as they flew with their white wings before the breeze, and apostrophizing them as animated by the living spirit of freedom. Who can read that passage, and be insensible to its pathos and sublimity? Compressed into it is a whole Alexandrian library of thought, feeling, and sentiment—all that can, all that need be urged, in the form of expostulation, entreaty, rebuke, against that crime of crimes,—making man the property of his fellow-man! O, how accursed is that system, which entombs the godlike mind of man, defaces the divine image, reduces those who by creation were crowned with glory and honor to a level with four-footed beasts, and exalts the dealer in human flesh above all that is called God! Why should its existence be prolonged one hour? Is it not evil, only evil, and that continually? What does its presence imply but the absence of all fear of God, all regard for man, on the part of the people of the United States? Heaven speed its eternal overthrow!

So profoundly ignorant of the nature of slavery are many persons, that they are stubbornly incredulous whenever they read or listen to any recital of the cruelties which are daily inflicted on its victims. They do not deny that the slaves are held as property; but that terrible fact seems to convey to their minds no idea of injustice, exposure to outrage, or savage barbarity. Tell them of cruel scourgings, of mutilations and brandings, of scenes of pollution and blood, of the banishment of all light and knowledge, and they affect to be greatly indignant at such enormous exaggerations, such wholesale misstatements, such abominable libels on the character of the southern planters! As if all these direful outrages were not the natural results of slavery! As if it were less cruel to reduce a human being to the condition of a thing, than to give him a severe flagellation, or to deprive him of necessary food and clothing! As if whips, chains, thumb-screws, paddles, bloodhounds, overseers, drivers, patrols, were not all indispensable to keep the slaves down, and to give protection to their ruthless oppressors! As if, when the marriage institution is abolished, concubinage, adultery, and incest, must not necessarily abound; when all the rights of humanity are annihilated, any barrier remains to protect the victim from the fury of the spoiler; when absolute power is assumed over life and liberty, it will not be wielded with destructive sway! Skeptics of this character abound in society. In some few instances, their incredulity arises from a want of reflection; but, generally, it indicates a hatred of the light, a desire to shield slavery from the assaults of its foes, a contempt of the colored race, whether bond or free. Such will try to discredit the shocking tales of slaveholding cruelty which are recorded in this truthful Narrative; but they will labor in vain. Mr. DOUGLASS has frankly disclosed the place of his birth, the names of those who claimed ownership in his body and soul, and the names also of those who committed the crimes which he has alleged against them. His statements, therefore, may easily be disproved, if they are untrue.

In the course of his Narrative, he relates two instances of murderous cruelty,—in one of which a planter deliberately shot a slave belonging to a neighboring plantation, who had unintentionally gotten within his lordly domain in quest of fish; and in the other, an overseer blew out the brains of a slave who had fled to a stream of water to escape a bloody scourging. Mr. DOUGLASS states that in neither of these instances was any thing done by way of legal arrest or judicial investigation. The Baltimore American, of March 17, 1845, relates a similar case of atrocity, perpetrated with similar impunity—as follows:— "*Shooting a Slave.*—We learn, upon the authority of a letter from Charles county, Maryland, received by a gentleman of this city, that a young man, named Matthews, a nephew of General Matthews, and whose father, it is believed, holds an office at Washington, killed one of the slaves upon his father's farm by shooting him. The letter states that young Matthews had been left in charge of the farm; that he gave an order to the servant, which was disobeyed, when he proceeded to the house, *obtained a gun, and, returning, shot the servant.* He immediately, the letter continues, fled to his father's residence, where he still remains unmolested."—Let it never be forgotten, that no slaveholder or overseer can be convicted of any outrage perpetrated on the person of a slave, however diabolical it may be, on the testimony of colored witnesses, whether bond or free. By the slave code, they are adjudged to be as incompetent to testify against a white man, as though they were indeed a part of the brute creation. Hence, there is no legal protection in fact, whatever there may be in form, for the slave population; and any amount of cruelty may be inflicted on them with impunity. Is it possible for the human mind to conceive of a more horrible state of society?

The effect of a religious profession on the conduct of southern masters is vividly described in the following Narrative, and shown to be any thing but salutary. In the nature of the case, it must be in the highest degree pernicious. The testimony of Mr. DOUGLASS, on this point, is sustained by a cloud of witnesses, whose veracity is unimpeachable. "A slaveholder's profession of Christianity is a palpable imposture. He is a felon of the highest grade. He is a man-stealer. It is of no importance what you put in the other scale."

Reader! are you with the man-stealers in sympathy and purpose, or on the side of their down-trodden victims? If with the former, then are you the foe of God and man. If with the latter, what are you prepared to do and dare in their behalf? Be faithful, be vigilant, be untiring in your efforts to break every yoke, and let the oppressed go free. Come what may—cost what it may—inscribe on the banner which you unfurl to the breeze, as your religious and political motto—"NO COMPROMISE WITH SLAVERY! NO UNION WITH SLAVEHOLDERS!"

WM. LLOYD GARRISON

BOSTON, *May* 1, 1845

LETTER FROM WENDELL PHILLIPS, ESQ.

BOSTON, *April* 22, 1845

MY DEAR FRIEND:

You remember the old fable of "The Man and the Lion," where the lion complained that he should not be so misrepresented "when the lions wrote history."

I am glad the time has come when the "lions write history." We have been left long enough to gather the character of slavery from the involuntary evidence of the masters. One might, indeed, rest sufficiently satisfied with what, it is evident, must be, in general, the results of such a relation, without seeking farther to find whether they have followed in every instance. Indeed, those who stare at the half-peck of corn a week, and love to count the lashes on the slave's back, are seldom the "stuff" out of which reformers and abolitionists are to be made. I remember that, in 1838, many were waiting for the results of the West India experiment, before they could come into our ranks. Those "results" have come long ago; but, alas! few of that number have come with them, as converts. A man must be disposed to judge of emancipation by other tests than whether it has increased the produce of sugar,—and to hate slavery for other reasons than because it starves men and whips women,—before he is ready to lay the first stone of his anti-slavery life.

I was glad to learn, in your story, how early the most neglected of God's children waken to a sense of their rights, and of the injustice done them. Experience is a keen teacher; and long before you had mastered your A B C, or knew where the "white sails" of the Chesapeake were bound, you began, I see, to gauge the wretchedness of the slave, not by his hunger and want, not by his lashes and toil, but by the cruel and blighting death which gathers over his soul.

In connection with this, there is one circumstance which makes your recollections peculiarly valuable, and renders your early insight the more remarkable. You come from that part of the country where we are told slavery appears with its fairest features. Let us hear, then, what it is at its best estate—gaze on its bright side, if it has one; and then imagination may task her powers to add dark lines to the picture, as she travels southward to that (for the colored man) Valley of the Shadow of Death, where the Mississippi sweeps along.

Again, we have known you long, and can put the most entire confidence in your truth, candor, and sincerity. Every one who has heard you speak has felt, and, I am confident, every one who reads your book will feel, persuaded that you give them a fair specimen of the whole truth. No one-sided portrait,—no wholesale complaints,—but strict justice done, whenever individual kindliness has neutralized, for a moment, the deadly system with which it was strangely allied. You have been with us, too, some years, and can fairly compare the twilight of rights, which your race enjoy at the North, with that "noon of night" under which they labor south of Mason and Dixon's line. Tell us whether, after all, the half-free colored man of Massachusetts is worse off than the pampered slave of the rice swamps!

In reading your life, no one can say that we have unfairly picked out some rare specimens of cruelty. We know that the bitter drops, which even you have drained from the cup, are no incidental aggravations, no individual ills, but such as must mingle always and necessarily in the lot of every slave. They are the essential ingredients, not the occasional results, of the system.

After all, I shall read your book with trembling for you. Some years ago, when you were beginning to tell me your real name and birthplace, you may remember I stopped you, and preferred to remain ignorant of all. With the exception of a vague description, so I continued, till the other day, when you read me your memoirs. I hardly knew, at the time, whether to thank you or not for the sight of them, when I reflected that it was still dangerous, in Massachusetts, for honest men to tell their names! They say the fathers, in 1776, signed the Declaration of Independence with the halter about their necks. You, too, publish your declaration of freedom with danger compassing you around. In all the broad lands which the Constitution of the United States overshadows, there is no single spot,—however narrow or desolate,—where a fugitive slave can plant himself and say, "I am safe." The whole armory of Northern Law has no shield for you. I am free to say that, in your place, I should throw the MS. into the fire.

You, perhaps, may tell your story in safety, endeared as you are to so many warm hearts by rare gifts, and a still rarer devotion of them to the service of others. But it will be owing only to your labors, and the fearless efforts of those who, trampling the laws and Constitution of the country under their feet, are determined that they will "hide the outcast," and that their hearths shall be, spite of the law, an asylum for the oppressed, if, some time or other, the humblest may stand in our streets, and bear witness in safety against the cruelties of which he has been the victim.

Yet it is sad to think, that these very throbbing hearts which welcome your story, and form your best safeguard in telling it, are all beating contrary to the "statute in such case made and provided." Go on, my dear friend, till you, and those who, like you, have been saved, so as by fire, from the dark prison-house, shall stereotype these free, illegal pulses into statutes; and New England, cutting loose from a blood-stained Union, shall glory in being the house of refuge for the oppressed;—till we no longer merely "*hide* the outcast," or make a merit of standing idly by while he is hunted in our midst; but, consecrating anew the soil of the Pilgrims as an asylum for the oppressed, proclaim our *welcome* to the slave so loudly, that the tones shall reach every hut in the Carolinas, and make the broken-hearted bondman leap up at the thought of old Massachusetts.

God speed the day!

Till then, and ever,

Yours truly,

WENDELL PHILLIPS

FREDERICK DOUGLASS

CHAPTER I

I WAS BORN in Tuckahoe, near Hillsborough, and about twelve miles from Easton, in Talbot county, Maryland. I have no accurate knowledge of my age, never having seen any authentic record containing it. By far the larger part of the slaves know as little of their ages as horses know of theirs, and it is the wish of most masters within my knowledge to keep their slaves thus ignorant. I do not remember to have ever met a slave who could tell of his birthday. They seldom come nearer to it than planting-time, harvest-time, cherry-time, spring-time, or fall-time. A want of information concerning my own was a source of unhappiness to me even during childhood. The white children could tell their ages. I could not tell why I ought to be deprived of the same privilege. I was not allowed to make any inquiries of my master concerning it. He deemed all such inquiries on the part of a slave improper and impertinent, and evidence of a restless spirit. The nearest estimate I can give makes me now between twenty-seven and twenty-eight years of age. I come to this, from hearing my master say, some time during 1835, I was about seventeen years old.

My mother was named Harriet Bailey. She was the daughter of Isaac and Betsey Bailey, both colored, and quite dark. My mother was of a darker complexion than either my grandmother or grandfather.

My father was a white man. He was admitted to be such by all I ever heard speak of my parentage. The opinion was also whispered that my master was my father; but of the correctness of this opinion, I know nothing; the means of knowing was withheld from me. My mother and I were separated when I was but an infant—before I knew her as my mother. It is a common custom, in the part of Maryland from which I ran away, to part children from their mothers at a very early age. Frequently, before the child has reached its twelfth month, its mother is taken from it, and hired out on some farm a considerable distance off, and the child is placed under the care of an old woman, too old for field labor. For what this separation is done, I do not know, unless it be to hinder the development of the child's affection toward its mother, and to blunt and destroy the natural affection of the mother for the child. This is the inevitable result.

I never saw my mother, to know her as such, more than four or five times in my life; and each of these times was very short in duration, and at night. She was hired by a Mr. Stewart, who lived about twelve miles from my home. She made her journeys to see me in the night, travelling the whole distance on foot, after the performance of her day's work. She was a field hand, and a whipping is the penalty of not being in the field at sunrise, unless a slave has special permission from his or her master to the contrary—a permission which they seldom get, and one that gives to him that gives it the proud name of being a kind master. I do not recollect of ever seeing my mother by the light of day. She was with me in the night. She would lie down with me, and get me to sleep, but long before I waked she was gone. Very little communication ever took place between us. Death soon ended what little we could have while she lived, and with it her hardships and suffering. She died when I was about seven years old, on one of my master's farms, near Lee's Mill. I was not allowed to be present during her illness, at her death, or burial. She was gone long before I knew any thing about it. Never having enjoyed, to any considerable extent, her soothing presence, her tender and watchful care, I received the tidings of her death with much the same emotions I should have probably felt at the death of a stranger.

Called thus suddenly away, she left me without the slightest intimation of who my father was. The whisper that my master was my father, may or may not be true; and, true or false, it is of but little consequence to my purpose whilst the fact remains, in all its glaring odiousness, that slaveholders have ordained, and by law established, that the children of slave women shall in all cases follow the condition of their mothers; and this is done too obviously to administer to their own lusts, and make a gratification of their wicked desires profitable as well as pleasurable; for by this cunning arrangement, the slaveholder, in cases not a few, sustains to his slaves the double relation of master and father.

I know of such cases; and it is worthy of remark that such slaves invariably suffer greater hardships, and have more to contend with, than others. They are, in the first place, a constant offence to their mistress. She is ever disposed to find fault with them; they can seldom do any thing to please her; she is never better pleased than when she sees them under the lash, especially when she suspects her husband of showing to his mulatto children favors which he withholds from his black slaves. The master is frequently compelled to sell this class of his slaves, out of deference to the feelings of his white wife; and, cruel as the deed may strike any one to be, for a man to sell his own children to human flesh-mongers, it is often the dictate of humanity for him to do so; for, unless he does this, he must not only whip them himself, but must stand by and see one white son tie up his brother, of but few shades darker complexion than himself, and ply the gory lash to his naked back; and if he lisp one word of disapproval, it is set down to his parental partiality, and only makes a bad matter worse, both for himself and the slave whom he would protect and defend.

Every year brings with it multitudes of this class of slaves. It was doubtless in consequence of a knowledge of this fact, that one great statesman of the south predicted the downfall of slavery by the inevitable laws of population. Whether this prophecy is ever fulfilled or not, it is nevertheless plain that a very different-looking class of people are springing up at the south, and are now held in slavery, from those originally brought to this country from Africa; and if their increase will do no other good, it will do away the force of the argument, that God cursed Ham, and therefore American slavery is right. If the lineal descendants of Ham are alone to be scripturally enslaved, it is certain that slavery at the south must soon become unscriptural; for thousands are ushered into the world, annually, who, like myself, owe their existence to white fathers, and those fathers most frequently their own masters.

I have had two masters. My first master's name was Anthony. I do not remember his first name. He was generally called Captain Anthony—a title which, I presume, he acquired by sailing a craft on the Chesapeake Bay. He was not considered a rich slaveholder. He owned two or three farms, and about thirty slaves. His farms and slaves were under the care of an overseer. The overseer's name was Plummer. Mr. Plummer was a miserable drunkard, a profane swearer, and a savage monster. He always went armed with a cowskin and a heavy cudgel. I have known him to cut and slash the womens heads so horribly, that even master would be enraged at his cruelty, and would threaten to whip him if he did not mind himself. Master, however, was not a humane slaveholder. It required extraordinary barbarity on the part of an overseer to affect him. He was a cruel man, hardened by a long life of slaveholding. He would at times seem to take great pleasure in whipping a slave. I have often been awakened at the dawn of day by the most heart-rending shrieks of an own aunt of mine, whom he used to tie up to a joist, and whip upon her naked back till she was literally covered with blood. No words, no tears, no prayers, from his gory victim, seemed to move his iron heart from its bloody purpose. The louder she screamed, the harder he whipped; and where the blood ran fastest, there he whipped longest. He would whip her to make her scream, and whip her to make her hush; and not until overcome by fatigue, would he cease to swing the blood-clotted cowskin. I remember the first time I ever witnessed this horrible exhibition. I was quite a child, but I well remember it. I never shall forget it whilst I remember any thing. It was the first of a long series of such outrages, of which I was doomed to be a witness and a participant. It struck me with awful force. It was the blood-stained gate, the entrance to the hell of slavery, through which I was about to pass. It was a most terrible spectacle. I wish I could commit to paper the feelings with which I beheld it.

This occurrence took place very soon after I went to live with my old master, and under the following circumstances. Aunt Hester went out one night,—where or for what I do not know,—and happened to be absent when my master desired her presence. He had ordered her not to go out evenings, and warned her that she must never let him catch her in company with a young man, who was paying attention to her, belonging to Colonel Lloyd. The young man's name was Ned Roberts, generally called Lloyd's Ned. Why master was so careful of her, may be safely left to conjecture. She was a woman of noble form, and of graceful proportions, having very few equals, and fewer superiors, in personal appearance, among the colored or white women of our neighborhood.

Aunt Hester had not only disobeyed his orders in going out, but had been found in company with Lloyd's Ned; which circumstance, I found, from what he said while whipping her, was the chief offence. Had he been a man of pure morals himself, he might have been thought interested in protecting the innocence of my aunt; but those who knew him will not suspect him of any such virtue. Before he commenced whipping Aunt Hester, he took her into the kitchen, and stripped her from neck to waist, leaving her neck, shoulders, and back, entirely naked. He then told her to cross her hands, calling her at the same time a d——d b——h. After crossing her hands, he tied them with a strong rope, and led her to a stool under a large hook in the joist, put in for the purpose. He made her get upon the stool, and tied her hands to the hook. She now stood fair for his infernal purpose. Her arms were stretched up at their full length, so that she stood upon the ends of her toes. He then said to her, "Now, you d——d b——h, I'll learn you how to disobey my orders!" and after rolling up his sleeves, he commenced to lay on the heavy cowskin, and soon the warm, red blood (amid heartrending shrieks from her, and horrid oaths from him) came dripping to the floor. I was so terrified and horror-stricken at the sight, that I hid myself in a closet, and dared not venture out till long after the bloody transaction was over. I expected it would be my turn next. It was all new to me. I had never seen any thing like it before. I had always lived with my grandmother on the outskirts of the plantation, where she was put to raise the children of the younger women. I had therefore been, until now, out of the way of the bloody scenes that often occurred on the plantation.

Chapter II

My master's family consisted of two sons, Andrew and Richard; one daughter, Lucretia, and her husband, Captain Thomas Auld. They lived in one house, upon the home plantation of Colonel Edward Lloyd. My master was Colonel Lloyd's clerk and superintendent. He was what might be called the overseer of the overseers. I spent two years of childhood on this plantation in my old master's family. It was here that I witnessed the bloody transaction recorded in the first chapter; and as I received my first impressions of slavery on this plantation, I will give some description of it, and of slavery as it there existed. The plantation is about twelve miles north of Easton, in Talbot county, and is situated on the border of Miles River. The principal products raised upon it were tobacco, corn, and wheat. These were raised in great abundance; so that, with the products of this and the other farms belonging to him, he was able to keep in almost constant employment a large sloop, in carrying them to market at Baltimore. This sloop was named Sally Lloyd, in honor of one of the colonel's daughters. My master's son-in-law, Captain Auld, was master of the vessel; she was otherwise manned by the colonel's own slaves. Their names were Peter, Isaac, Rich, and Jake. These were esteemed very highly by the other slaves, and looked upon as the privileged ones of the plantation; for it was no small affair, in the eyes of the slaves, to be allowed to see Baltimore.

Colonel Lloyd kept from three to four hundred slaves on his home plantation, and owned a large number more on the neighboring farms belonging to him. The names of the farms nearest to the home plantation were Wye Town and New Design. "Wye Town" was under the overseership of a man named Noah Willis. New Design was under the overseership of a Mr. Townsend. The overseers of these, and all the rest of the farms, numbering over twenty, received advice and direction from the managers of the home plantation. This was the great business place. It was the seat of government for the whole twenty farms. All disputes among the overseers were settled here. If a slave was convicted of any high misdemeanor, became unmanageable, or evinced a determination to run away, he was brought immediately here, severely whipped, put on board the sloop, carried to Baltimore, and sold to Austin Woolfolk, or some other slave-trader, as a warning to the slaves remaining.

Here, too, the slaves of all the other farms received their monthly allowance of food, and their yearly clothing. The men and women slaves received, as their monthly allowance of food, eight pounds of pork, or its equivalent in fish, and one bushel of corn meal. Their yearly clothing consisted of two coarse linen shirts, one pair of linen trousers, like the shirts, one jacket, one pair of trousers for winter, made of coarse negro cloth, one pair of stockings, and one pair of shoes; the whole of which could not have cost more than seven dollars. The allowance of the slave children was given to their mothers, or the old women having the care of them. The children unable to work in the field had neither shoes, stockings, jackets, nor trousers, given to them; their clothing consisted of two coarse linen shirts per year. When these failed them, they went naked until the next allowance-day. Children from seven to ten years old, of both sexes, almost naked, might be seen at all seasons of the year.

There were no beds given the slaves, unless one coarse blanket be considered such, and none but the men and women had these. This, however, is not considered a very great privation. They find less difficulty from the want of beds, than from the want of time to sleep; for when their day's work in the field is done, the most of them having their washing, mending, and cooking to do, and having few or none of the ordinary facilities for doing either of these, very many of their sleeping hours are consumed in preparing for the field the coming day; and when this is done, old and young, male and female, married and single, drop down side by side, on one common bed,—the cold, damp floor,—each covering himself or herself with their miserable blankets; and here they sleep till they are summoned to the field by the driver's horn. At the sound of this, all must rise, and be off to the field. There must be no halting; every one must be at his or her post; and woe betides them who hear not this morning summons to the field; for if they are not awakened by the sense of hearing, they are by the sense of feeling: no age nor sex finds any favor. Mr. Severe, the overseer, used to stand by the door of the quarter, armed with a large hickory stick and heavy cowskin, ready to whip any one who was so unfortunate as not to hear, or, from any other cause, was prevented from being ready to start for the field at the sound of the horn.

Mr. Severe was rightly named: he was a cruel man. I have seen him whip a woman, causing the blood to run half an hour at the time; and this, too, in the midst of her crying children, pleading for their mother's release. He seemed to take pleasure in manifesting his fiendish barbarity. Added to his cruelty, he was a profane swearer. It was enough to chill the blood and stiffen the hair of an ordinary man to hear him talk. Scarce a sentence escaped him but that was commenced or concluded by some horrid oath. The field was the place to witness his cruelty and profanity. His presence made it both the field of blood and of blasphemy. From the rising till the going down of the sun, he was cursing, raving, cutting, and slashing among the slaves of the field, in the most frightful manner. His career was short. He died very soon after I went to Colonel Lloyd's; and he died as he lived, uttering, with his dying groans, bitter curses and horrid oaths. His death was regarded by the slaves as the result of a merciful providence.

Mr. Severe's place was filled by a Mr. Hopkins. He was a very different man. He was less cruel, less profane, and made less noise, than Mr. Severe. His course was characterized by no extraordinary demonstrations of cruelty. He whipped, but seemed to take no pleasure in it. He was called by the slaves a good overseer.

The home plantation of Colonel Lloyd wore the appearance of a country village. All the mechanical operations for all the farms were performed here. The shoemaking and mending, the blacksmithing, cartwrighting, coopering, weaving, and grain-grinding, were all performed by the slaves on the home plantation. The whole place wore a business-like aspect very unlike the neighboring farms. The number of houses, too, conspired to give it advantage over the neighboring farms. It was called by the slaves the *Great House Farm*. Few privileges were esteemed higher, by the slaves of the out-farms, than that of being selected to do errands at the Great House Farm. It was associated in their minds with greatness. A representative could not be prouder of his election to a seat in the American Congress, than a slave on one of the out-farms would be of his election to do errands at the Great House Farm. They regarded it as evidence of great confidence reposed in them by their overseers; and it was on this account, as well as a constant desire to be out of the field from under the driver's lash, that they esteemed it a high privilege, one worth careful living for. He was called the smartest and most trusty fellow, who had this honor conferred upon him the most frequently. The competitors for this office sought as diligently to please their overseers, as the office-seekers in the political parties seek to please and deceive the people. The same traits of character might be seen in Colonel Lloyd's slaves, as are seen in the slaves of the political parties.

The slaves selected to go to the Great House Farm, for the monthly allowance for themselves and their fellow-slaves, were peculiarly enthusiastic. While on their way, they would make the dense old woods, for miles around, reverberate with their wild songs, revealing at once the highest joy and the deepest sadness. They would compose and sing as they went along, consulting neither time nor tune. The thought that came up, came out—if not in the word, in the sound;—and as frequently in the one as in the other. They would sometimes sing the most pathetic sentiment in the most rapturous tone, and the most rapturous sentiment in the most pathetic tone. Into all of their songs they would manage to weave something of the Great House Farm. Especially would they do this, when leaving home. They would then sing most exultingly the following words:—

> "I am going away to the Great House Farm!
> O, yea! O, yea! O!"

This they would sing, as a chorus, to words which to many would seem unmeaning jargon, but which, nevertheless, were full of meaning to themselves. I have sometimes thought that the mere hearing of those songs would do more to impress some minds with the horrible character of slavery, than the reading of whole volumes of philosophy on the subject could do.

I did not, when a slave, understand the deep meaning of those rude and apparently incoherent songs. I was myself within the circle; so that I neither saw nor heard as those without might see and hear. They told a tale of woe which was then altogether beyond my feeble comprehension; they were tones loud, long, and deep; they breathed the prayer and complaint of souls boiling over with the bitterest anguish. Every tone was a testimony against slavery, and a prayer to God for deliverance from chains. The hearing of those wild notes always depressed my spirit, and filled me with ineffable sadness. I have frequently found myself in tears while hearing them. The mere recurrence to those songs, even now, afflicts me; and while I am writing these lines, an expression of feeling has already found its way down my cheek. To those songs I trace my first glimmering conception of the dehumanizing character of slavery. I can never get rid of that conception. Those songs still follow me, to deepen my hatred of slavery, and quicken my sympathies for my brethren in bonds. If any one wishes to be impressed with the soul-killing effects of slavery, let him go to Colonel Lloyd's plantation, and, on allowance-day, place himself in the deep pine woods, and there let him, in silence, analyze the sounds that shall pass through the chambers of his soul,—and if he is not thus impressed, it will only be because "there is no flesh in his obdurate heart."

I have often been utterly astonished, since I came to the north, to find persons who could speak of the singing, among slaves, as evidence of their contentment and happiness. It is impossible to conceive of a greater mistake. Slaves sing most when they are most unhappy. The songs of the slave represent the sorrows of his heart; and he is relieved by them, only as an aching heart is relieved by its tears. At least, such is my experience. I have often sung to drown my sorrow, but seldom to express my happiness. Crying for joy, and singing for joy, were alike uncommon to me while in the jaws of slavery. The singing of a man cast away upon a desolate island might be as appropriately considered as evidence of contentment and happiness, as the singing of a slave; the songs of the one and of the other are prompted by the same emotion.

Chapter III

Colonel Lloyd kept a large and finely cultivated garden, which afforded almost constant employment for four men, besides the chief gardener, (Mr. M'Durmond.) This garden was probably the greatest attraction of the place. During the summer months, people came from far and near—from Baltimore, Easton, and Annapolis—to see it. It abounded in fruits of almost every description, from the hardy apple of the north to the delicate orange of the south. This garden was not the least source of trouble on the plantation. Its excellent fruit was quite a temptation to the hungry swarms of boys, as well as the older slaves, belonging to the colonel, few of whom had the virtue or the vice to resist it. Scarcely a day passed, during the summer, but that some slave had to take the lash for stealing fruit. The colonel had to resort to all kinds of stratagems to keep his slaves out of the garden. The last and most successful one was that of tarring his fence all around; after which, if a slave was caught with any tar upon his person, it was deemed sufficient proof that he had either been into the garden, or had tried to get in. In either case, he was severely whipped by the chief gardener. This plan worked well; the slaves became as fearful of tar as of the lash. They seemed to realize the impossibility of touching *tar* without being defiled.

The colonel also kept a splendid riding equipage. His stable and carriage-house presented the appearance of some of our large city livery establishments. His horses were of the finest form and noblest blood. His carriage-house contained three splendid coaches, three or four gigs, besides dearborns and barouches of the most fashionable style.

This establishment was under the care of two slaves—old Barney and young Barney—father and son. To attend to this establishment was their sole work. But it was by no means an easy employment; for in nothing was Colonel Lloyd more particular than in the management of his horses. The slightest inattention to these was unpardonable, and was visited upon those, under whose care they were placed, with the severest punishment; no excuse could shield them, if the colonel only suspected any want of attention to his horses—a supposition which he frequently indulged, and one which, of course, made the office of old and young Barney a very trying one. They never knew when they were safe from punishment. They were frequently whipped when least deserving, and escaped whipping when most deserving it. Every thing depended upon the looks of the horses, and the state of Colonel Lloyd's own mind when his horses were brought to him for use. If a horse did not move fast enough, or hold his head high enough, it was owing to some fault of his keepers. It was painful to stand near the stable-door, and hear the various complaints against the keepers when a horse was taken out for use. "This horse has not had proper attention. He has not been sufficiently rubbed and curried, or he has not been properly fed; his food was too wet or too dry; he got it too soon or too late; he was too hot or too cold; he had too much hay, and not enough of grain; or he had too much grain, and not enough of hay; instead of old Barney's attending to the horse, he had very improperly left it to his son." To all these complaints, no matter how unjust, the slave must answer never a word. Colonel Lloyd could not brook any contradiction from a slave. When he spoke, a slave must stand, listen, and tremble; and such was literally the case. I have seen Colonel Lloyd make old Barney, a man between fifty and sixty years of age, uncover his bald head, kneel down upon the cold, damp ground, and receive upon his naked and toil-worn shoulders more than thirty lashes at the time. Colonel Lloyd had three sons—Edward, Murray, and Daniel,—and three sons-in-law, Mr. Winder, Mr. Nicholson, and Mr. Lowndes. All of these lived at the Great House Farm, and enjoyed the luxury of whipping the servants when they pleased, from old Barney down to William Wilkes, the coach-driver. I have seen Winder make one of the house-servants stand off from him a suitable distance to be touched with the end of his whip, and at every stroke raise great ridges upon his back.

To describe the wealth of Colonel Lloyd would be almost equal to describing the riches of Job. He kept from ten to fifteen house-servants. He was said to own a thousand slaves, and I think this estimate quite within the truth. Colonel Lloyd owned so many that he did not know them when he saw them; nor did all the slaves of the out-farms know him. It is reported of him, that, while riding along the road one day, he met a colored man, and addressed him in the usual manner of speaking to colored people on the public highways of the south: "Well, boy, whom do you belong to?" "To Colonel Lloyd," replied the slave. "Well, does the colonel treat you well?" "No, sir," was the ready reply. "What, does he work you too hard?" "Yes, sir." "Well, don't he give you enough to eat?" "Yes, sir, he gives me enough, such as it is."

The colonel, after ascertaining where the slave belonged, rode on; the man also went on about his business, not dreaming that he had been conversing with his master. He thought, said, and heard nothing more of the matter, until two or three weeks afterwards. The poor man was then informed by his overseer that, for having found fault with his master, he was now to be sold to a Georgia trader. He was immediately chained and handcuffed; and thus, without a moment's warning, he was snatched away, and forever sundered, from his family and friends, by a hand more unrelenting than death. This is the penalty of

telling the truth, of telling the simple truth, in answer to a
series of plain questions.

It is partly in consequence of such facts, that slaves, when
inquired of as to their condition and the character of their masters, almost universally say they are contented, and that their
masters are kind. The slaveholders have been known to send in
spies among their slaves, to ascertain their views and feelings
in regard to their condition. The frequency of this has had the
effect to establish among the slaves the maxim, that a still
tongue makes a wise head. They suppress the truth rather than
take the consequences of telling it, and in so doing prove themselves a part of the human family. If they have any thing to say
of their masters, it is generally in their masters' favor, especially when speaking to an untried man. I have been frequently
asked, when a slave, if I had a kind master, and do not remember
ever to have given a negative answer; nor did I, in pursuing this
course, consider myself as uttering what was absolutely false;
for I always measured the kindness of my master by the standard
of kindness set up among slaveholders around us. Moreover,
slaves are like other people, and imbibe prejudices quite common
to others. They think their own better than that of others. Many,
under the influence of this prejudice, think their own masters
are better than the masters of other slaves; and this, too, in some
cases, when the very reverse is true. Indeed, it is not uncommon
for slaves even to fall out and quarrel among themselves about
the relative goodness of their masters, each contending for the
superior goodness of his own over that of the others. At the very
same time, they mutually execrate their masters when viewed
separately. It was so on our plantation. When Colonel Lloyd's
slaves met the slaves of Jacob Jepson, they seldom parted without
a quarrel about their masters; Colonel Lloyd's slaves contending
that he was the richest, and Mr. Jepson's slaves that he was the
smartest, and most of a man. Colonel Lloyd's slaves would boast
his ability to buy and sell Jacob Jepson. Mr. Jepson's slaves
would boast his ability to whip Colonel Lloyd. These quarrels

would almost always end in a fight between the parties, and those that whipped were supposed to have gained the point at issue. They seemed to think that the greatness of their masters was transferable to themselves. It was considered as being bad enough to be a slave; but to be a poor man's slave was deemed a disgrace indeed!

Chapter IV

Mr. Hopkins remained but a short time in the office of overseer. Why his career was so short, I do not know, but suppose he lacked the necessary severity to suit Colonel Lloyd. Mr. Hopkins was succeeded by Mr. Austin Gore, a man possessing, in an eminent degree, all those traits of character indispensable to what is called a first-rate overseer. Mr. Gore had served Colonel Lloyd, in the capacity of overseer, upon one of the out-farms, and had shown himself worthy of the high station of overseer upon the home or Great House Farm.

Mr. Gore was proud, ambitious, and persevering. He was artful, cruel, and obdurate. He was just the man for such a place, and it was just the place for such a man. It afforded scope for the full exercise of all his powers, and he seemed to be perfectly at home in it. He was one of those who could torture the slightest look, word, or gesture, on the part of the slave, into impudence, and would treat it accordingly. There must be no answering back to him; no explanation was allowed a slave, showing himself to have been wrongfully accused. Mr. Gore acted fully up to the maxim laid down by slaveholders,—"It is better that a dozen slaves suffer under the lash, than that the overseer should be convicted, in the presence of the slaves, of having been at fault." No matter how innocent a slave might be—it availed him nothing, when accused by Mr. Gore of any misdemeanor. To be accused was to be convicted, and to be convicted was to be punished; the one always following the other with immutable certainty. To escape punishment was to escape accusation; and few slaves had the fortune to do either, under the overseership of Mr. Gore. He was just proud enough to demand the most debasing homage of the slave, and quite servile enough to crouch, himself, at the feet of the master. He was ambitious enough to be contented with nothing short of the highest rank of overseers, and persevering enough to reach the height of his ambition. He was cruel enough to inflict the severest punishment, artful enough to descend to the lowest trickery, and obdurate enough to be insensible to the voice of a reproving conscience. He was, of all the overseers, the most dreaded by the slaves. His presence was painful; his eye flashed confusion; and seldom was his sharp, shrill voice heard, without producing horror and trembling in their ranks.

Mr. Gore was a grave man, and, though a young man, he indulged in no jokes, said no funny words, seldom smiled. His words were in perfect keeping with his looks, and his looks were in perfect keeping with his words. Overseers will sometimes indulge in a witty word, even with the slaves; not so with Mr. Gore. He spoke but to command, and commanded but to be obeyed; he dealt sparingly with his words, and bountifully with his whip, never using the former where the latter would answer as well. When he whipped, he seemed to do so from a sense of duty, and feared no consequences. He did nothing reluctantly, no matter how disagreeable; always at his post, never inconsistent. He never promised but to fulfill. He was, in a word, a man of the most inflexible firmness and stone-like coolness.

His savage barbarity was equalled only by the consummate coolness with which he committed the grossest and most savage deeds upon the slaves under his charge. Mr. Gore once undertook to whip one of Colonel Lloyd's slaves, by the name of Demby. He had given Demby but few stripes, when, to get rid of the scourging, he ran and plunged himself into a creek, and stood there at the depth of his shoulders, refusing to come out. Mr. Gore told him that he would give him three calls, and that, if he did not come out at the third call, he would shoot him. The first call was given. Demby made no response, but stood his ground. The second and third calls were given with the same result. Mr. Gore then, without consultation or deliberation with any one, not even giving Demby an additional call, raised his musket to his face, taking deadly aim at his standing victim, and in an instant poor Demby was no more. His mangled body sank out of sight, and blood and brains marked the water where he had stood.

A thrill of horror flashed through every soul upon the plantation, excepting Mr. Gore. He alone seemed cool and collected. He was asked by Colonel Lloyd and my old master, why he resorted to this extraordinary expedient. His reply was, (as well as I can remember,) that Demby had become unmanageable. He was setting a dangerous example to the other slaves,—one which, if suffered to pass without some such demonstration on his part, would finally lead to the total subversion of all rule and order upon the plantation. He argued that if one slave refused to be corrected, and escaped with his life, the other slaves would soon copy the example; the result of which would be, the freedom of the slaves, and the enslavement of the whites. Mr. Gore's defence was satisfactory. He was continued in his station as overseer upon the home plantation. His fame as an overseer went abroad. His horrid crime was not even submitted to judicial investigation. It was committed in the presence of slaves, and they of course could neither institute a suit, nor testify against him; and thus the guilty perpetrator of one of the bloodiest and most foul murders goes unwhipped of justice, and uncensured by the community in which he lives. Mr. Gore lived in St. Michael's, Talbot county, Maryland, when I left there; and if he is still alive, he very probably lives there now; and if so, he is now, as he was then, as highly esteemed and as much respected as though his guilty soul had not been stained with his brother's blood.

I speak advisedly when I say this,—that killing a slave, or any colored person, in Talbot county, Maryland, is not treated as a crime, either by the courts or the community. Mr. Thomas Lanman, of St. Michael's, killed two slaves, one of whom he killed with a hatchet, by knocking his brains out. He used to boast of the commission of the awful and bloody deed. I have heard him do so laughingly, saying, among other things, that he was the only benefactor of his country in the company, and that when others would do as much as he had done, we should be relieved of "the d——d niggers."

The wife of Mr. Giles Hick, living but a short distance from where I used to live, murdered my wife's cousin, a young girl between fifteen and sixteen years of age, mangling her person in the most horrible manner, breaking her nose and breastbone with a stick, so that the poor girl expired in a few hours afterward. She was immediately buried, but had not been in her untimely grave but a few hours before she was taken up and examined by the coroner, who decided that she had come to her death by severe beating. The offence for which this girl was thus murdered was this:—She had been set that night to mind Mrs. Hick's baby, and during the night she fell asleep, and the baby cried. She, having lost her rest for several nights previous, did not hear the crying. They were both in the room with Mrs. Hicks. Mrs. Hicks, finding the girl slow to move, jumped from her bed, seized an oak stick of wood by the fireplace, and with it broke the girl's nose and breastbone, and thus ended her life. I will not say that this most horrid murder produced no sensation in the community. It did produce sensation, but not enough to bring the murderess to punishment. There was a warrant issued for her arrest, but it was never served. Thus she escaped not only punishment, but even the pain of being arraigned before a court for her horrid crime.

Whilst I am detailing bloody deeds which took place during my stay on Colonel Lloyd's plantation, I will briefly narrate another, which occurred about the same time as the murder of Demby by Mr. Gore.

Colonel Lloyd's slaves were in the habit of spending a part of their nights and Sundays in fishing for oysters, and in this way made up the deficiency of their scanty allowance. An old man belonging to Colonel Lloyd, while thus engaged, happened to get beyond the limits of Colonel Lloyd's, and on the premises of Mr. Beal Bondly. At this trespass, Mr. Bondly took offence, and with his musket came down to the shore, and blew its deadly contents into the poor old man.

Mr. Bondly came over to see Colonel Lloyd the next day, whether to pay him for his property, or to justify himself in what he had done, I know not. At any rate, this whole fiendish transaction was soon hushed up. There was very little said about it at all, and nothing done. It was a common saying, even among little white boys, that it was worth a half-cent to kill a "nigger," and a half-cent to bury one.

Chapter V

As to my own treatment while I lived on Colonel Lloyd's plantation, it was very similar to that of the other slave children. I was not old enough to work in the field, and there being little else than field work to do, I had a great deal of leisure time. The most I had to do was to drive up the cows at evening, keep the fowls out of the garden, keep the front yard clean, and run of errands for my old master's daughter, Mrs. Lucretia Auld. The most of my leisure time I spent in helping Master Daniel Lloyd in finding his birds, after he had shot them. My connection with Master Daniel was of some advantage to me. He became quite attached to me, and was a sort of protector of me. He would not allow the older boys to impose upon me, and would divide his cakes with me.

I was seldom whipped by my old master, and suffered little from any thing else than hunger and cold. I suffered much from hunger, but much more from cold. In hottest summer and coldest winter, I was kept almost naked—no shoes, no stockings, no jacket, no trousers, nothing on but a coarse tow linen shirt, reaching only to my knees. I had no bed. I must have perished with cold, but that, the coldest nights, I used to steal a bag which was used for carrying corn to the mill. I would crawl into this bag, and there sleep on the cold, damp, clay floor, with my head in and feet out. My feet have been so cracked with the frost, that the pen with which I am writing might be laid in the gashes.

We were not regularly allowanced. Our food was coarse corn meal boiled. This was called *mush*. It was put into a large wooden tray or trough, and set down upon the ground. The children were then called, like so many pigs, and like so many pigs they would come and devour the mush; some with oyster-shells, others with pieces of shingle, some with naked hands, and none with spoons. He that ate fastest got most; he that was strongest secured the best place; and few left the trough satisfied.

I was probably between seven and eight years old when I left Colonel Lloyd's plantation. I left it with joy. I shall never forget the ecstasy with which I received the intelligence that my old master (Anthony) had determined to let me go to Baltimore, to live with Mr. Hugh Auld, brother to my old master's son-in-law, Captain Thomas Auld. I received this information about three days before my departure. They were three of the happiest days I ever enjoyed. I spent the most part of all these three days in the creek, washing off the plantation scurf, and preparing myself for my departure.

The pride of appearance which this would indicate was not my own. I spent the time in washing, not so much because I wished to, but because Mrs. Lucretia had told me I must get all the dead skin off my feet and knees before I could go to Baltimore; for the people in Baltimore were very cleanly, and would laugh at me if I looked dirty. Besides, she was going to give me a pair of trousers, which I should not put on unless I got all the dirt off me. The thought of owning a pair of trousers was great indeed! It was almost a sufficient motive, not only to make me take off what would be called by pig-drovers the mange, but the skin itself. I went at it in good earnest, working for the first time with the hope of reward.

The ties that ordinarily bind children to their homes were all suspended in my case. I found no severe trial in my departure. My home was charmless; it was not home to me; on parting from it, I could not feel that I was leaving any thing which I could have enjoyed by staying. My mother was dead, my grand-mother lived far off, so that I seldom saw her. I had two sisters and one brother, that lived in the same house with me; but the early separation of us from our mother had well nigh blotted the fact of our relationship from our memories. I looked for home elsewhere, and was confident of finding none which I should relish less than the one which I was leaving. If, however, I found in my new home hardship, hunger, whipping, and nakedness, I had the consolation that I should not have escaped any one of them by staying. Having already had more than a taste of them in the house of my old master, and having endured them there, I very naturally inferred my ability to endure them elsewhere, and especially at Baltimore; for I had something of the feeling about Baltimore that is expressed in the proverb, that "being hanged in England is preferable to dying a natural death in Ireland." I had the strongest desire to see Baltimore. Cousin Tom, though not fluent in speech, had inspired me with that desire by his eloquent description of the place. I could never point out any thing at the Great House, no matter how beautiful or powerful, but that he had seen something at Baltimore far exceeding, both in beauty and strength, the object which I pointed out to him. Even the Great House itself, with all its pictures, was far inferior to many buildings in Baltimore. So strong was my desire, that I thought a gratification of it would fully compensate for whatever loss of comforts I should sustain by the exchange. I left without a regret, and with the highest hopes of future happiness.

We sailed out of Miles River for Baltimore on a Saturday morning. I remember only the day of the week, for at that time I had no knowledge of the days of the month, nor the months of the year. On setting sail, I walked aft, and gave to Colonel Lloyd's plantation what I hoped would be the last look. I then placed myself in the bows of the sloop, and there spent the remainder of the day in looking ahead, interesting myself in what was in the distance rather than in things near by or behind.

In the afternoon of that day, we reached Annapolis, the capital of the State. We stopped but a few moments, so that I had no time to go on shore. It was the first large town that I had ever seen, and though it would look small compared with some of our New England factory villages, I thought it a wonderful place for its size—more imposing even than the Great House Farm!

We arrived at Baltimore early on Sunday morning, landing at Smith's Wharf, not far from Bowley's Wharf. We had on board the sloop a large flock of sheep; and after aiding in driving them to the slaughter-house of Mr. Curtis on Louden Slater's Hill, I was conducted by Rich, one of the hands belonging on board of the sloop, to my new home in Alliciana Street, near Mr. Gardner's ship-yard, on Fells Point.

Mr. and Mrs. Auld were both at home, and met me at the door with their little son Thomas, to take care of whom I had been given. And here I saw what I had never seen before; it was a white face beaming with the most kindly emotions; it was the face of my new mistress, Sophia Auld. I wish I could describe the rapture that flashed through my soul as I beheld it. It was a new and strange sight to me, brightening up my pathway with the light of happiness. Little Thomas was told, there was his Freddy,—and I was told to take care of little Thomas; and thus I entered upon the duties of my new home with the most cheering prospect ahead.

I look upon my departure from Colonel Lloyd's plantation as one of the most interesting events of my life. It is possible, and even quite probable, that but for the mere circumstance of being removed from that plantation to Baltimore, I should have to-day, instead of being here seated by my own table, in the enjoyment of freedom and the happiness of home, writing this Narrative, been confined in the galling chains of slavery. Going to live at Baltimore laid the foundation, and opened the gateway, to all my subsequent prosperity. I have ever regarded it as the first plain manifestation of that kind providence which has ever since attended me, and marked my life with so many favors. I regarded the selection of myself as being somewhat remarkable. There were a number of slave children that might have been sent from the plantation to Baltimore. There were those younger, those older, and those of the same age. I was chosen from among them all, and was the first, last, and only choice.

I may be deemed superstitious, and even egotistical, in regarding this event as a special interposition of divine Providence in my favor. But I should be false to the earliest sentiments of my soul, if I suppressed the opinion. I prefer to be true to myself, even at the hazard of incurring the ridicule of others, rather than to be false, and incur my own abhorrence. From my earliest recollection, I date the entertainment of a deep conviction that slavery would not always be able to hold me within its foul embrace; and in the darkest hours of my career in slavery, this living word of faith and spirit of hope departed not from me, but remained like ministering angels to cheer me through the gloom. This good spirit was from God, and to him I offer thanksgiving and praise.

Chapter VI

My new mistress proved to be all she appeared when I first met her at the door,—a woman of the kindest heart and finest feelings. She had never had a slave under her control previously to myself, and prior to her marriage she had been dependent upon her own industry for a living. She was by trade a weaver; and by constant application to her business, she had been in a good degree preserved from the blighting and dehumanizing effects of slavery. I was utterly astonished at her goodness. I scarcely knew how to behave towards her. She was entirely unlike any other white woman I had ever seen. I could not approach her as I was accustomed to approach other white ladies. My early instruction was all out of place. The crouching servility, usually so acceptable a quality in a slave, did not answer when manifested toward her. Her favor was not gained by it; she seemed to be disturbed by it. She did not deem it impudent or unmannerly for a slave to look her in the face. The meanest slave was put fully at ease in her presence, and none left without feeling better for having seen her. Her face was made of heavenly smiles, and her voice of tranquil music.

But, alas! this kind heart had but a short time to remain such. The fatal poison of irresponsible power was already in her hands, and soon commenced its infernal work. That cheerful eye, under the influence of slavery, soon became red with rage; that voice, made all of sweet accord, changed to one of harsh and horrid discord; and that angelic face gave place to that of a demon.

Very soon after I went to live with Mr. and Mrs. Auld, she very kindly commenced to teach me the A, B, C. After I had learned this, she assisted me in learning to spell words of three or four letters. Just at this point of my progress, Mr. Auld found out what was going on, and at once forbade Mrs. Auld to instruct me further, telling her, among other things, that it was unlawful, as well as unsafe, to teach a slave to read. To use his own words, further, he said, "If you give a nigger an inch, he will take an ell. A nigger should know nothing but to obey his master—to do as he is told to do. Learning would *spoil* the best nigger in the world. Now," said he, "if you teach that nigger (speaking of myself) how to read, there would be no keeping him. It would forever unfit him to be a slave. He would at once become unmanageable, and of no value to his master. As to himself, it could do him no good, but a great deal of harm. It would make him discontented and unhappy." These words sank deep into my heart, stirred up sentiments within that lay slumbering, and called into existence an entirely new train of thought. It was a new and special revelation, explaining dark and mysterious things, with which my youthful understanding had struggled, but struggled in vain. I now understood what had been to me a most perplexing difficulty—to wit, the white man's power to enslave the black man. It was a grand achievement, and I prized it highly. From that moment, I understood the pathway from slavery to freedom. It was just what I wanted, and I got it at a time when I the least expected it. Whilst I was saddened by the thought of losing the aid of my kind mistress, I was gladdened by the invaluable instruction which, by the merest accident, I had gained from my master. Though conscious of the difficulty of learning without a teacher, I set out with high hope, and a fixed purpose, at whatever cost of trouble, to learn how to read. The very decided manner with which he spoke, and strove to impress his wife with the evil consequences of giving me instruction, served to convince me that he was deeply sensible of the truths he was uttering. It gave me the best assurance that I might rely with the utmost confidence on the results which, he said, would flow from teaching me to read. What he most dreaded, that I most desired. What he most loved, that I most hated. That which to him was a great evil, to be carefully shunned, was to me a great good, to be diligently sought; and the argument which he so warmly urged, against my learning to read, only served to inspire me with a desire and determination to learn. In learning to read, I owe almost as much to the bitter opposition of my master, as to the kindly aid of my mistress. I acknowledge the benefit of both.

I had resided but a short time in Baltimore before I observed a marked difference, in the treatment of slaves, from that which I had witnessed in the country. A city slave is almost a freeman, compared with a slave on the plantation. He is much better fed and clothed, and enjoys privileges altogether unknown to the slave on the plantation. There is a vestige of decency, a sense of shame, that does much to curb and check those outbreaks of atrocious cruelty so commonly enacted upon the plantation. He is a desperate slaveholder, who will shock the humanity of his non-slaveholding neighbors with the cries of his lacerated slave. Few are willing to incur the odium attaching to the reputation of being a cruel master; and above all things, they would not be known as not giving a slave enough to eat. Every city slave-holder is anxious to have it known of him, that he feeds his slaves well; and it is due to them to say, that most of them do give their slaves enough to eat. There are, however, some painful exceptions to this rule. Directly opposite to us, on Philpot Street, lived Mr. Thomas Hamilton. He owned two slaves. Their names were Henrietta and Mary. Henrietta was about twenty-two years of age, Mary was about fourteen; and of all the mangled and emaciated creatures I ever looked upon, these two were the most so. His heart must be harder than stone, that could look upon these unmoved. The head, neck, and shoulders of Mary were literally cut to pieces. I have frequently felt her head, and found it nearly covered with festering sores, caused by the lash of her cruel mistress. I do not know that her master ever whipped her, but I have been an eye-witness to the cruelty of Mrs. Hamilton.

I used to be in Mr. Hamilton's house nearly every day. Mrs. Hamilton used to sit in a large chair in the middle of the room, with a heavy cowskin always by her side, and scarce an hour passed during the day but was marked by the blood of one of these slaves. The girls seldom passed her without her saying, "Move faster, you *black gip!*" at the same time giving them a blow with the cowskin over the head or shoulders, often drawing the blood. She would then say, "Take that, you *black gip!*"— continuing, "If you don't move faster, I'll move you!" Added to the cruel lashings to which these slaves were subjected, they were kept nearly half-starved. They seldom knew what it was to eat a full meal. I have seen Mary contending with the pigs for the offal thrown into the street. So much was Mary kicked and cut to pieces, that she was oftener called "*pecked*" than by her name.

Chapter VII

I LIVED IN Master Hugh's family about seven years. During this time, I succeeded in learning to read and write. In accomplishing this, I was compelled to resort to various stratagems. I had no regular teacher. My mistress, who had kindly commenced to instruct me, had, in compliance with the advice and direction of her husband, not only ceased to instruct, but had set her face against my being instructed by any one else. It is due, however, to my mistress to say of her, that she did not adopt this course of treatment immediately. She at first lacked the depravity indispensable to shutting me up in mental darkness. It was at least necessary for her to have some training in the exercise of irresponsible power, to make her equal to the task of treating me as though I were a brute.

My mistress was, as I have said, a kind and tender-hearted woman; and in the simplicity of her soul she commenced, when I first went to live with her, to treat me as she supposed one human being ought to treat another. In entering upon the duties of a slaveholder, she did not seem to perceive that I sustained to her the relation of a mere chattel, and that for her to treat me as a human being was not only wrong, but dangerously so. Slavery proved as injurious to her as it did to me. When I went there, she was a pious, warm, and tender-hearted woman. There was no sorrow or suffering for which she had not a tear. She had bread for the hungry, clothes for the naked, and comfort for every mourner that came within her reach. Slavery soon proved its ability to divest her of these heavenly qualities. Under its influence, the tender heart became stone, and the lamblike

51

disposition gave way to one of tiger-like fierceness. The first step in her downward course was in her ceasing to instruct me. She now commenced to practise her husband's precepts. She finally became even more violent in her opposition than her husband himself. She was not satisfied with simply doing as well as he had commanded; she seemed anxious to do better. Nothing seemed to make her more angry than to see me with a newspaper. She seemed to think that here lay the danger. I have had her rush at me with a face made all up of fury, and snatch from me a newspaper, in a manner that fully revealed her apprehension. She was an apt woman; and a little experience soon demonstrated, to her satisfaction, that education and slavery were incompatible with each other.

From this time I was most narrowly watched. If I was in a separate room any considerable length of time, I was sure to be suspected of having a book, and was at once called to give an account of myself. All this, however, was too late. The first step had been taken. Mistress, in teaching me the alphabet, had given me the *inch*, and no precaution could prevent me from taking the *ell*.

The plan which I adopted, and the one by which I was most successful, was that of making friends of all the little white boys whom I met in the street. As many of these as I could, I converted into teachers. With their kindly aid, obtained at different times and in different places, I finally succeeded in learning to read. When I was sent of errands, I always took my book with me, and by going one part of my errand quickly, I found time to get a lesson before my return. I used also to carry bread with me, enough of which was always in the house, and to which I was always welcome; for I was much better off in this regard than many of the poor white children in our neighborhood. This bread I used to bestow upon the hungry little urchins, who, in return, would give me that more valuable bread of knowledge. I am strongly tempted to give the names of two or three of those little boys, as a testimonial of the gratitude and affection I bear them; but prudence forbids;—not that it would injure me, but it might embarrass them; for it is almost an unpardonable offence to teach slaves to read in this Christian country. It is enough to say of the dear little fellows, that they lived on Philpot Street, very near Durgin and Bailey's ship-yard. I used to talk this matter of slavery over with them. I would sometimes say to them, I wished I could be as free as they would be when they got to be men. "You will be free as soon as you are twenty-one, *but I am a slave for life!* Have not I as good a right to be free as you have?" These words used to trouble them; they would express for me the liveliest sympathy, and console me with the hope that something would occur by which I might be free.

I was now about twelve years old, and the thought of being *a slave for life* began to bear heavily upon my heart. Just about this time, I got hold of a book entitled "The Columbian Orator." Every opportunity I got, I used to read this book. Among much of other interesting matter, I found in it a dialogue between a master and his slave. The slave was represented as having run away from his master three times. The dialogue represented the conversation which took place between them, when the slave was retaken the third time. In this dialogue, the whole argument in behalf of slavery was brought forward by the master, all of which was disposed of by the slave. The slave was made to say some very smart as well as impressive things in reply to his master—things which had the desired though unexpected effect; for the conversation resulted in the voluntary emancipation of the slave on the part of the master.

In the same book, I met with one of Sheridan's mighty speeches on and in behalf of Catholic emancipation. These were choice documents to me. I read them over and over again with unabated interest. They gave tongue to interesting thoughts of my own soul, which had frequently flashed through my mind, and died away for want of utterance. The moral which I gained from the dialogue was the power of truth over the conscience of even a slaveholder. What I got from Sheridan was a bold denunciation of slavery, and a powerful vindication of human rights. The reading of these documents enabled me to utter my thoughts, and to meet the arguments brought forward to sustain slavery; but while they relieved me of one difficulty, they brought on another even more painful than the one of which I was relieved. The more I read, the more I was led to abhor and detest my enslavers. I could regard them in no other light than a band of successful robbers, who had left their homes, and gone to Africa, and stolen us from our homes, and in a strange land reduced us to slavery. I loathed them as being the meanest as well as the most wicked of men. As I read and contemplated the subject, behold! that very discontentment which Master Hugh had predicted would follow my learning to read had already come, to torment and sting my soul to unutterable anguish. As I writhed under it, I would at times feel that learning to read had been a curse rather than a blessing. It had given me a view of my wretched condition, without the remedy. It opened my eyes to the horrible pit, but to no ladder upon which to get out. In moments of agony, I envied my fellow-slaves for their stupidity. I have often wished myself a beast. I preferred the condition of the meanest reptile to my own. Any thing, no matter what, to get rid of thinking! It was this everlasting thinking of my condition that tormented me. There was no getting rid of it. It was pressed upon me by every object within sight or hearing, animate or inanimate. The silver trump of freedom had roused my soul to eternal wakefulness. Freedom now appeared, to disappear no more forever. It was heard in every sound, and seen in every thing. It was ever present to torment me with a sense of my wretched condition. I saw nothing without seeing it, I heard nothing without hearing it, and felt nothing without feeling it. It looked from every star, it smiled in every calm, breathed in every wind, and moved in every storm.

I often found myself regretting my own existence, and wishing myself dead; and but for the hope of being free, I have no doubt but that I should have killed myself, or done something for which I should have been killed. While in this state of mind, I was eager to hear any one speak of slavery. I was a ready listener. Every little while, I could hear something about the abolitionists. It was some time before I found what the word meant. It was always used in such connections as to make it an interesting word to me. If a slave ran away and succeeded in getting clear, or if a slave killed his master, set fire to a barn, or did any thing very wrong in the mind of a slaveholder, it was spoken of as the fruit of *abolition*. Hearing the word in this connection very often, I set about learning what it meant. The dictionary afforded me little or no help. I found it was "the act of abolishing;" but then I did not know what was to be abolished. Here I was perplexed. I did not dare to ask any one about its meaning, for I was satisfied that it was something they wanted me to know very little about. After a patient waiting, I got one of our city papers, containing an account of the number of petitions from the north, praying for the abolition of slavery in the District of Columbia, and of the slave trade between the States. From this time I understood the words *abolition* and *abolitionist*, and always drew near when that word was spoken, expecting to hear something of importance to myself and fellow-slaves. The light broke in upon me by degrees. I went one day down on the wharf of Mr. Waters; and seeing two Irishmen unloading a scow of stone, I went, unasked, and helped them. When we had finished, one of them came to me and asked me if I were a slave. I told him I was. He asked, "Are ye a slave for life?" I told him that I was. The good Irishman seemed to be deeply affected by the statement. He said to the other that it was a pity so fine a little fellow as myself should be a slave for life. He said it was a shame to hold me. They both advised me to run away to the north; that I should find friends there, and that I should be free. I pretended not to be interested in what they said, and treated them as if I did not understand them; for I feared they might be treacherous. White men have been known to encourage slaves to escape, and then, to get the reward, catch them and return them to their masters. I was afraid that these seemingly good men might use me so; but I nevertheless remembered their advice, and from that time I resolved to run away. I looked forward to a time at which it would be safe for me to escape. I was too young to think of doing so immediately; besides, I wished to learn how to write, as I might have occasion to write my own pass. I consoled myself with the hope that I should one day find a good chance. Meanwhile, I would learn to write.

The idea as to how I might learn to write was suggested to me by being in Durgin and Bailey's ship-yard, and frequently seeing the ship carpenters, after hewing, and getting a piece of timber ready for use, write on the timber the name of that part of the ship for which it was intended. When a piece of timber was intended for the larboard side, it would be marked thus— "L." When a piece was for the starboard side, it would be marked thus—"S." A piece for the larboard side forward, would be marked thus—"L. F." When a piece was for starboard side forward, it would be marked thus—"S. F." For larboard aft, it would be marked thus—"L. A." For starboard aft, it would be marked thus—"S. A." I soon learned the names of these letters, and for what they were intended when placed upon a piece of timber in the ship-yard. I immediately commenced copying them, and in a short time was able to make the four letters named. After that, when I met with any boy who I knew could write, I would tell him I could write as well as he. The next word would be, "I don't believe you. Let me see you try it." I would then make the letters which I had been so fortunate as to learn, and ask him to beat that. In this way I got a good many lessons in writing, which it is quite possible I should never have gotten in any other way. During this time, my copy-book was the board fence, brick wall, and pavement; my pen and ink was a lump of chalk. With these, I learned mainly how to write. I then commenced and continued copying the Italics in Webster's Spelling Book, until I could make them all without looking on the book. By this time, my little Master Thomas had gone to school, and learned how to write, and had written over a number of copy-books. These had been brought home, and shown to some of our near neighbors, and then laid aside. My mistress used to go to class meeting at the Wilk Street meeting-house every Monday afternoon, and leave me to take care of the house. When left thus, I used to spend the time in writing in the spaces left in Master Thomas's copy-book, copying what he had written. I continued to do this until I could write a hand very similar to that of Master Thomas. Thus, after a long, tedious effort for years, I finally succeeded in learning how to write.

Chapter VIII

In a very short time after I went to live at Baltimore, my old master's youngest son Richard died; and in about three years and six months after his death, my old master, Captain Anthony, died, leaving only his son, Andrew, and daughter, Lucretia, to share his estate. He died while on a visit to see his daughter at Hillsborough. Cut off thus unexpectedly, he left no will as to the disposal of his property. It was therefore necessary to have a valuation of the property, that it might be equally divided between Mrs. Lucretia and Master Andrew. I was immediately sent for, to be valued with the other property. Here again my feelings rose up in detestation of slavery. I had now a new conception of my degraded condition. Prior to this, I had become, if not insensible to my lot, at least partly so. I left Baltimore with a young heart overborne with sadness, and a soul full of apprehension. I took passage with Captain Rowe, in the schooner Wild Cat, and, after a sail of about twenty-four hours, I found myself near the place of my birth. I had now been absent from it almost, if not quite, five years. I, however, remembered the place very well. I was only about five years old when I left it, to go and live with my old master on Colonel Lloyd's plantation; so that I was now between ten and eleven years old.

We were all ranked together at the valuation. Men and women, old and young, married and single, were ranked with horses, sheep, and swine. There were horses and men, cattle and women, pigs and children, all holding the same rank in the scale of being, and were all subjected to the same narrow examination. Silvery-headed age and sprightly youth, maids and matrons, had to undergo the same indelicate inspection. At this moment, I saw more clearly than ever the brutalizing effects of slavery upon both slave and slaveholder.

After the valuation, then came the division. I have no language to express the high excitement and deep anxiety which were felt among us poor slaves during this time. Our fate for life was now to be decided. We had no more voice in that decision than the brutes among whom we were ranked. A single word from the white men was enough—against all our wishes, prayers, and entreaties—to sunder forever the dearest friends, dearest kindred, and strongest ties known to human beings. In addition to the pain of separation, there was the horrid dread of falling into the hands of Master Andrew. He was known to us all as being a most cruel wretch,—a common drunkard, who had, by his reckless mismanagement and profligate dissipation, already wasted a large portion of his father's property. We all felt that we might as well be sold at once to the Georgia traders, as to pass into his hands; for we knew that that would be our inevitable condition,—a condition held by us all in the utmost horror and dread.

I suffered more anxiety than most of my fellow-slaves. I had known what it was to be kindly treated; they had known nothing of the kind. They had seen little or nothing of the world. They were in very deed men and women of sorrow, and acquainted with grief. Their backs had been made familiar with the bloody lash, so that they had become callous; mine was yet tender; for while at Baltimore I got few whippings, and few slaves could boast of a kinder master and mistress than myself; and the thought of passing out of their hands into those of Master Andrew—a man who, but a few days before, to give me a sample of his bloody disposition, took my little brother by the throat, threw him on the ground, and with the heel of his boot stamped upon his head till the blood gushed from his nose and ears—was well calculated to make me anxious as to my fate. After he had committed this savage outrage upon my brother, he turned to me, and said that was the way he meant to serve me one of these days,—meaning, I suppose, when I came into his possession.

Thanks to a kind Providence, I fell to the portion of Mrs. Lucretia, and was sent immediately back to Baltimore, to live again in the family of Master Hugh. Their joy at my return equalled their sorrow at my departure. It was a glad day to me. I had escaped a worse than lion's jaws. I was absent from Baltimore, for the purpose of valuation and division, just about one month, and it seemed to have been six.

Very soon after my return to Baltimore, my mistress, Lucretia, died, leaving her husband and one child, Amanda; and in a very short time after her death, Master Andrew died. Now all the property of my old master, slaves included, was in the hands of strangers,—strangers who had had nothing to do with accumulating it. Not a slave was left free. All remained slaves, from the youngest to the oldest. If any one thing in my experience, more than another, served to deepen my conviction of the infernal character of slavery, and to fill me with unutterable loathing of slaveholders, it was their base ingratitude to my poor old grandmother. She had served my old master faithfully from youth to old age. She had been the source of all his wealth; she had peopled his plantation with slaves; she had become a great grandmother in his service. She had rocked him in infancy, attended him in childhood, served him through life, and at his death wiped from his icy brow the cold death-sweat, and closed his eyes forever. She was nevertheless left a slave—a slave for life—a slave in the hands of strangers; and in their hands she saw her children, her grandchildren, and her great-grandchildren, divided, like so many sheep, without being gratified with the small privilege of a single word, as to their or her own destiny. And, to cap the climax of their base ingratitude and fiendish barbarity, my grandmother, who was now very old, having outlived my old master and all his children, having seen the beginning and end of all of them, and her present owners finding she was of but little value, her frame already racked with the pains of old age, and complete helplessness fast stealing over her once active limbs, they took her to the woods, built her a little hut, put up a little mud-chimney, and then made her welcome to the privilege of supporting herself there in perfect loneliness; thus virtually turning her out to die! If my poor old grandmother now lives, she lives to suffer in utter loneliness; she lives to remember and mourn over the loss of children, the loss of grandchildren, and the loss of great-grandchildren. They are, in the language of the slave's poet, Whittier,—

> "Gone, gone, sold and gone
> To the rice swamp dank and lone,
> Where the slave-whip ceaseless swings,
> Where the noisome insect stings,
> Where the fever-demon strews
> Poison with the falling dews,
> Where the sickly sunbeams glare
> Through the hot and misty air:—
>   Gone, gone, sold and gone
>   To the rice swamp dank and lone,
>   From Virginia hills and waters—
>   Woe is me, my stolen daughters!"

The hearth is desolate. The children, the unconscious children, who once sang and danced in her presence, are gone. She gropes her way, in the darkness of age, for a drink of water. Instead of the voices of her children, she hears by day the moans of the dove, and by night the screams of the hideous owl. All is gloom. The grave is at the door. And now, when weighed down by the pains and aches of old age, when the head inclines to the feet, when the beginning and ending of human existence meet, and helpless infancy and painful old age combine together—at this time, this most needful time, the time for the exercise of that tenderness and affection which children only can exercise towards a declining parent—my poor old grandmother, the devoted mother of twelve children, is left all alone, in yonder little hut, before a few dim embers. She stands—she sits—she staggers—she falls—she groans—she dies—and there are none of her children or grandchildren present, to wipe from her wrinkled brow the cold sweat of death, or to place beneath the sod her fallen remains. Will not a righteous God visit for these things?

In about two years after the death of Mrs. Lucretia, Master Thomas married his second wife. Her name was Rowena Hamilton. She was the eldest daughter of Mr. William Hamilton. Master now lived in St. Michael's. Not long after his marriage, a misunderstanding took place between himself and Master Hugh; and as a means of punishing his brother, he took me from him to live with himself at St. Michael's. Here I underwent another most painful separation. It, however, was not so severe as the one I dreaded at the division of property; for, during this interval, a great change had taken place in Master Hugh and his once kind and affectionate wife. The influence of brandy upon him, and of slavery upon her, had effected a disastrous change in the characters of both; so that, as far as they were concerned, I thought I had little to lose by the change. But it was not to them that I was attached. It was to those little Baltimore boys that I felt the strongest attachment. I had received many good lessons from them, and was still receiving them, and the thought of leaving them was painful indeed. I was leaving, too, without the hope of ever being allowed to return. Master Thomas had said he would never let me return again. The barrier betwixt himself and brother he considered impassable.

I then had to regret that I did not at least make the attempt to carry out my resolution to run away; for the chances of success are tenfold greater from the city than from the country.

I sailed from Baltimore for St. Michael's in the sloop Amanda, Captain Edward Dodson. On my passage, I paid particular attention to the direction which the steamboats took to go to Philadelphia. I found, instead of going down, on reaching North Point they went up the bay, in a north-easterly direction. I deemed this knowledge of the utmost importance. My determination to run away was again revived. I resolved to wait only so long as the offering of a favorable opportunity. When that came, I was determined to be off.

CHAPTER IX

I HAVE NOW reached a period of my life when I can give dates. I left Baltimore, and went to live with Master Thomas Auld, at St. Michael's, in March, 1832. It was now more than seven years since I lived with him in the family of my old master, on Colonel Lloyd's plantation. We of course were now almost entire strangers to each other. He was to me a new master, and I to him a new slave. I was ignorant of his temper and disposition; he was equally so of mine. A very short time, however, brought us into full acquaintance with each other. I was made acquainted with his wife not less than with himself. They were well matched, being equally mean and cruel. I was now, for the first time during a space of more than seven years, made to feel the painful gnawings of hunger—a something which I had not experienced before since I left Colonel Lloyd's plantation. It went hard enough with me then, when I could look back to no period at which I had enjoyed a sufficiency. It was tenfold harder after living in Master Hugh's family, where I had always had enough to eat, and of that which was good. I have said Master Thomas was a mean man. He was so. Not to give a slave enough to eat, is regarded as the most aggravated development of meanness even among slaveholders. The rule is, no matter how coarse the food, only let there be enough of it. This is the theory; and in the part of Maryland from which I came, it is the general practice,—though there are many exceptions. Master Thomas gave us enough of neither coarse nor fine food. There were four slaves of us in the kitchen—my sister Eliza, my aunt Priscilla, Henny, and myself; and we were allowed less than a half of a bushel of corn-meal per week, and very little else, either in the shape of meat or vegetables. It was not enough for us to subsist upon. We were therefore reduced to the wretched necessity of living at the expense of our neighbors. This we did by begging and stealing, whichever came handy in the time of need, the one being considered as legitimate as the other. A great many times have we poor creatures been nearly perishing with hunger, when food in abundance lay mouldering in the safe and smoke-house, and our pious mistress was aware of the fact; and yet that mistress and her husband would kneel every morning, and pray that God would bless them in basket and store!

Bad as all slaveholders are, we seldom meet one destitute of every element of character commanding respect. My master was one of this rare sort. I do not know of one single noble act ever performed by him. The leading trait in his character was mean-ness; and if there were any other element in his nature, it was made subject to this. He was mean; and, like most other mean men, he lacked the ability to conceal his meanness. Captain Auld was not born a slaveholder. He had been a poor man, master only of a Bay craft. He came into possession of all his slaves by marriage; and of all men, adopted slaveholders are the worst. He was cruel, but cowardly. He commanded without firmness. In the enforcement of his rules, he was at times rigid, and at times lax. At times, he spoke to his slaves with the firmness of Napoleon and the fury of a demon; at other times, he might well be mis-taken for an inquirer who had lost his way. He did nothing of himself. He might have passed for a lion, but for his ears. In all things noble which he attempted, his own meanness shone most conspicuous. His airs, words, and actions, were the airs, words, and actions of born slaveholders, and, being assumed, were awk-ward enough. He was not even a good imitator. He possessed all the disposition to deceive, but wanted the power. Having no resources within himself, he was compelled to be the copyist of many, and being such, he was forever the victim of inconsistency; and of consequence he was an object of contempt, and was held as such even by his slaves. The luxury of having slaves of his own to wait upon him was something new and unprepared for. He was a slaveholder without the ability to hold slaves. He found himself incapable of managing his slaves either by force, fear, or fraud. We seldom called him "master;" we generally called him "Captain Auld," and were hardly disposed to title him at all. I doubt not that our conduct had much to do with making him appear awkward, and of consequence fretful. Our want of reverence for him must have perplexed him greatly. He wished to have us call him master, but lacked the firmness necessary to command us to do so. His wife used to insist upon our calling him so, but to no purpose. In August, 1832, my master attended a Methodist camp-meeting held in the Bay-side, Talbot county, and there experienced religion. I indulged a faint hope that his conversion would lead him to emancipate his slaves, and that, if he did not do this, it would, at any rate, make him more kind and humane. I was disappointed in both these respects. It neither made him to be humane to his slaves, nor to emancipate them. If it had any effect on his character, it made him more cruel and hateful in all his ways; for I believe him to have been a much worse man after his conversion than before. Prior to his conversion, he relied upon his own depravity to shield and sustain him in his savage barbarity; but after his conversion, he found religious sanction and support for his slaveholding cruelty. He made the greatest pretensions to piety. His house was the house of prayer. He prayed morning, noon, and night. He very soon distinguished himself among his brethren, and was soon made a class-leader and exhorter. His activity in revivals was great, and he proved himself an instrument in the hands of the church in converting many souls. His house was the preachers' home. They used to take great pleasure in coming there to put up; for while he starved us, he stuffed them. We have had three or four preachers there at a time. The names of those who used to come most frequently while I lived there, were Mr. Storks, Mr. Ewery, Mr. Humphry, and Mr. Hickey. I have also seen Mr. George Cookman at our house. We slaves loved Mr. Cookman. We believed him to be a good man. We thought him instrumental in getting Mr. Samuel Harrison, a very rich slaveholder, to emancipate his slaves; and by some means got the impression that he was laboring to effect the emancipation of all the slaves. When he was at our house, we were sure to be called in to prayers. When the others were there, we were sometimes called in and sometimes not. Mr. Cookman took more notice of us than either of the other ministers. He could not come among us without betraying his sympathy for us, and, stupid as we were, we had the sagacity to see it.

While I lived with my master in St. Michael's, there was a white young man, a Mr. Wilson, who proposed to keep a Sabbath school for the instruction of such slaves as might be disposed to learn to read the New Testament. We met but three times, when Mr. West and Mr. Fairbanks, both class-leaders, with many others, came upon us with sticks and other missiles, drove us off, and forbade us to meet again. Thus ended our little Sabbath school in the pious town of St. Michael's.

I have said my master found religious sanction for his cruelty. As an example, I will state one of many facts going to prove the charge. I have seen him tie up a lame young woman, and whip her with a heavy cowskin upon her naked shoulders, causing the warm red blood to drip; and, in justification of the bloody deed, he would quote this passage of Scripture—"He that knoweth his master's will, and doeth it not, shall be beaten with many stripes."

Master would keep this lacerated young woman tied up in this horrid situation four or five hours at a time. I have known him to tie her up early in the morning, and whip her before breakfast; leave her, go to his store, return at dinner, and whip her again, cutting her in the places already made raw with his cruel lash. The secret of master's cruelty toward "Henny" is found in the fact of her being almost helpless. When quite a child, she fell into the fire, and burned herself horribly. Her hands were so burnt that she never got the use of them. She could do very little but bear heavy burdens. She was to master a bill of expense; and as he was a mean man, she was a constant offence to him. He seemed desirous of getting the poor girl out of existence. He gave her away once to his sister; but, being a poor gift, she was not disposed to keep her. Finally, my benevolent master, to use his own words, "set her adrift to take care of herself." Here was a recently-converted man, holding on upon the mother, and at the same time turning out her helpless child, to starve and die! Master Thomas was one of the many pious slaveholders who hold slaves for the very charitable purpose of taking care of them.

My master and myself had quite a number of differences. He found me unsuitable to his purpose. My city life, he said, had had a very pernicious effect upon me. It had almost ruined me for every good purpose, and fitted me for every thing which was bad. One of my greatest faults was that of letting his horse run away, and go down to his father-in-law's farm, which was about five miles from St. Michael's. I would then have to go after it. My reason for this kind of carelessness, or carefulness, was, that I could always get something to eat when I went there. Master William Hamilton, my master's father-in-law, always gave his slaves enough to eat. I never left there hungry, no matter how great the need of my speedy return. Master Thomas at length said he would stand it no longer. I had lived with him nine months, during which time he had given me a number of severe whippings, all to no good purpose. He resolved to put me out, as he said, to be broken; and, for this purpose, he let me for one year to a man named Edward Covey. Mr. Covey was a poor man, a farm-renter. He rented the place upon which he lived, as also the hands with which he tilled it. Mr. Covey had acquired a very high reputation for breaking young slaves, and this reputation was of immense value to him. It enabled him to get his farm tilled with much less expense to himself than he could have had it done without such a reputation. Some slaveholders thought it not much loss to allow Mr. Covey to have their slaves one year, for the sake of the training to which they were subjected, without any other compensation. He could hire young help with great ease, in consequence of this reputation. Added to the natural good qualities of Mr. Covey, he was a professor of religion—a pious soul—a member and a class-leader in the Methodist church. All of this added weight to his reputation as a "nigger-breaker." I was aware of all the facts, having been made acquainted with them by a young man who had lived there. I nevertheless made the change gladly; for I was sure of getting enough to eat, which is not the smallest consideration to a hungry man.

Chapter X

I LEFT MASTER THOMAS'S house, and went to live with Mr. Covey, on the 1st of January, 1833. I was now, for the first time in my life, a field hand. In my new employment, I found myself even more awkward than a country boy appeared to be in a large city. I had been at my new home but one week before Mr. Covey gave me a very severe whipping, cutting my back, causing the blood to run, and raising ridges on my flesh as large as my little finger. The details of this affair are as follows: Mr. Covey sent me, very early in the morning of one of our coldest days in the month of January, to the woods, to get a load of wood. He gave me a team of unbroken oxen. He told me which was the in-hand ox, and which the off-hand one. He then tied the end of a large rope around the horns of the in-hand ox, and gave me the other end of it, and told me, if the oxen started to run, that I must hold on upon the rope. I had never driven oxen before, and of course I was very awkward. I, however, succeeded in getting to the edge of the woods with little difficulty; but I had got a very few rods into the woods, when the oxen took fright, and started full tilt, carrying the cart against trees, and over stumps, in the most frightful manner. I expected every moment that my brains would be dashed out against the trees. After running thus for a considerable distance, they finally upset the cart, dashing it with great force against a tree, and threw themselves into a dense thicket. How I escaped death, I do not know. There I was, entirely alone, in a thick wood, in a place new to me. My cart was upset and shattered, my oxen were entangled among the young trees, and there was none to help me. After a long spell of effort, I succeeded in getting my cart righted, my oxen disentangled, and again yoked to the cart. I now proceeded with my team to the place where I had, the day before, been chopping wood, and loaded my cart pretty heavily, thinking in this way to tame my oxen. I then proceeded on my way home. I had now consumed one half of the day. I got out of the woods safely, and now felt out of danger. I stopped my oxen to open the woods gate; and just as I did so, before I could get hold of my ox-rope, the oxen again started, rushed through the gate, catching it between the wheel and the body of the cart, tearing it to pieces, and coming within a few inches of crushing me against the gate-post. Thus twice, in one short day, I escaped death by the merest chance. On my return, I told Mr. Covey what had happened, and how it happened. He ordered me to return to the woods again immediately. I did so, and he followed on after me. Just as I got into the woods, he came up and told me to stop my cart, and that he would teach me how to trifle away my time, and break gates. He then went to a large gum-tree, and with his axe cut three large switches, and, after trimming them up neatly with his pocket-knife, he ordered me to take off my clothes. I made him no answer, but stood with my clothes on. He repeated his order. I still made him no answer, nor did I move to strip myself. Upon this he rushed at me with the fierceness of a tiger, tore off my clothes, and lashed me till he had worn out his switches, cutting me so savagely as to leave the marks visible for a long time after. This whipping was the first of a number just like it, and for similar offences.

I lived with Mr. Covey one year. During the first six months, of that year, scarce a week passed without his whipping me. I was seldom free from a sore back. My awkwardness was almost always his excuse for whipping me. We were worked fully up to the point of endurance. Long before day we were up, our horses fed, and by the first approach of day we were off to the field with our hoes and ploughing teams. Mr. Covey gave us enough to eat, but scarce time to eat it. We were often less than five minutes taking our meals. We were often in the field from the first approach of day till its last lingering ray had left us; and at saving-fodder time, midnight often caught us in the field binding blades.

Covey would be out with us. The way he used to stand it, was this. He would spend the most of his afternoons in bed. He would then come out fresh in the evening, ready to urge us on with his words, example, and frequently with the whip. Mr. Covey was one of the few slaveholders who could and did work with his hands. He was a hard-working man. He knew by himself just what a man or a boy could do. There was no deceiving him. His work went on in his absence almost as well as in his presence; and he had the faculty of making us feel that he was ever present with us. This he did by surprising us. He seldom approached the spot where we were at work openly, if he could do it secretly. He always aimed at taking us by surprise. Such was his cunning, that we used to call him, among ourselves, "the snake." When we were at work in the cornfield, he would sometimes crawl on his hands and knees to avoid detection, and all at once he would rise nearly in our midst, and scream out, "Ha, ha! Come, come! Dash on, dash on!" This being his mode of attack, it was never safe to stop a single minute. His comings were like a thief in the night. He appeared to us as being ever at hand. He was under every tree, behind every stump, in every bush, and at every window, on the plantation. He would sometimes mount his horse, as if bound to St. Michael's, a distance of seven miles, and in half an hour afterwards you would see him coiled up in the corner of the wood-fence, watching every motion of the slaves. He would, for this purpose, leave his horse tied up in the woods. Again, he would sometimes walk up to us, and give us orders as though he was upon the point of starting on a long journey, turn his back upon us, and make as though he was going to the house to get ready; and, before he would get half way thither, he would turn short and crawl into a fence-corner, or behind some tree, and there watch us till the going down of the sun.

Mr. Covey's *forte* consisted in his power to deceive. His life was devoted to planning and perpetrating the grossest deceptions. Every thing he possessed in the shape of learning or religion, he made conform to his disposition to deceive. He seemed to think himself equal to deceiving the Almighty. He would make a short prayer in the morning, and a long prayer at night; and, strange as it may seem, few men would at times appear more devotional than he. The exercises of his family devotions were always commenced with singing; and, as he was a very poor singer himself, the duty of raising the hymn generally came upon me. He would read his hymn, and nod at me to commence. I would at times do so; at others, I would not. My non-compliance would almost always produce much confusion. To show himself independent of me, he would start and stagger through with his hymn in the most discordant manner. In this state of mind, he prayed with more than ordinary spirit. Poor man! such was his disposition, and success at deceiving, I do verily believe that he sometimes deceived himself into the solemn belief, that he was a sincere worshipper of the most high God; and this, too, at a time when he may be said to have been guilty of compelling his woman slave to commit the sin of adultery. The facts in the case are these: Mr. Covey was a poor man; he was just commencing in life; he was only able to buy one slave; and, shocking as is the fact, he bought her, as he said, for a *breeder*. This woman was named Caroline. Mr. Covey bought her from Mr. Thomas Lowe, about six miles from St. Michael's. She was a large, able-bodied woman, about twenty years old. She had already given birth to one child, which proved her to be just what he wanted. After buying her, he hired a married man of Mr. Samuel Harrison, to live with him one year; and him he used to fasten up with her every night! The result was, that, at the end of the year, the miserable woman gave birth to twins. At this result Mr. Covey seemed to be highly pleased, both with the man and the wretched woman. Such was his joy, and that of his wife, that nothing they could do for Caroline during her confinement was too good, or too hard, to be done. The children were regarded as being quite an addition to his wealth.

If at any one time of my life more than another, I was made to drink the bitterest dregs of slavery, that time was during the first six months of my stay with Mr. Covey. We were worked in all weathers. It was never too hot or too cold; it could never rain, blow, hail, or snow, too hard for us to work in the field. Work, work, work, was scarcely more the order of the day than of the night. The longest days were too short for him, and the shortest nights too long for him. I was somewhat unmanageable when I first went there, but a few months of this discipline tamed me. Mr. Covey succeeded in breaking me. I was broken in body, soul, and spirit. My natural elasticity was crushed, my intellect languished, the disposition to read departed, the cheerful spark that lingered about my eye died; the dark night of slavery closed in upon me; and behold a man transformed into a brute!

Sunday was my only leisure time. I spent this in a sort of beast-like stupor, between sleep and wake, under some large tree. At times I would rise up, a flash of energetic freedom would dart through my soul, accompanied with a faint beam of hope, that flickered for a moment, and then vanished. I sank down again, mourning over my wretched condition. I was sometimes prompted to take my life, and that of Covey, but was prevented by a combination of hope and fear. My sufferings on this plantation seem now like a dream rather than a stern reality.

Our house stood within a few rods of the Chesapeake Bay, whose broad bosom was ever white with sails from every quarter of the habitable globe. Those beautiful vessels, robed in purest white, so delightful to the eye of freemen, were to me so many shrouded ghosts, to terrify and torment me with thoughts of my wretched condition. I have often, in the deep stillness of a summer's Sabbath, stood all alone upon the lofty banks of that noble bay, and traced, with saddened heart and tearful eye, the countless number of sails moving off to the mighty ocean. The sight of these always affected me powerfully. My thoughts would compel utterance; and there, with no audience but the Almighty, I would pour out my soul's complaint, in my rude way, with an apostrophe to the moving multitude of ships:—

"You are loosed from your moorings, and are free; I am fast in my chains, and am a slave! You move merrily before the gentle gale, and I sadly before the bloody whip! You are freedom's swift-winged angels, that fly round the world; I am confined in bands of iron! O that I were free! O, that I were on one of your gallant decks, and under your protecting wing! Alas! betwixt me and you, the turbid waters roll. Go on, go on. O that I could also go! Could I but swim! If I could fly! O, why was I born a man, of whom to make a brute! The glad ship is gone; she hides in the dim distance. I am left in the hottest hell of unending slavery. O God, save me! God, deliver me! Let me be free! Is there any God? Why am I a slave? I will run away. I will not stand it. Get caught, or get clear, I'll try it. I had as well die with ague as the fever. I have only one life to lose. I had as well be killed running as die standing. Only think of it; one hundred miles straight north, and I am free! Try it? Yes! God helping me, I will. It cannot be that I shall live and die a slave. I will take to the water. This very bay shall yet bear me into freedom. The steamboats steered in a north-east course from North Point. I will do the same; and when I get to the head of the bay, I will turn my canoe adrift, and walk straight through Delaware into Pennsylvania. When I get there, I shall not be required to have a pass; I can travel without being disturbed. Let but the first opportunity offer, and, come what will, I am off. Meanwhile, I will try to bear up under the yoke. I am not the only slave in the world. Why should I fret? I can bear as much as any of them. Besides, I am but a boy, and all boys are bound to some one. It may be that my misery in slavery will only increase my happiness when I get free. There is a better day coming."

Thus I used to think, and thus I used to speak to myself; goaded almost to madness at one moment, and at the next reconciling myself to my wretched lot.

I have already intimated that my condition was much worse, during the first six months of my stay at Mr. Covey's, than in the last six. The circumstances leading to the change in Mr. Covey's course toward me form an epoch in my humble history. You have seen how a man was made a slave; you shall see how a slave was made a man. On one of the hottest days of the month of August, 1833, Bill Smith, William Hughes, a slave named Eli, and myself, were engaged in fanning wheat. Hughes was clearing the fanned wheat from before the fan, Eli was turning, Smith was feeding, and I was carrying wheat to the fan. The work was simple, requiring strength rather than intellect; yet, to one entirely unused to such work, it came very hard. About three o'clock of that day, I broke down; my strength failed me; I was seized with a violent aching of the head, attended with extreme dizziness; I trembled in every limb. Finding what was coming, I nerved myself up, feeling it would never do to stop work. I stood as long as I could stagger to the hopper with grain. When I could stand no longer, I fell, and felt as if held down by an immense weight. The fan of course stopped; every one had his own work to do; and no one could do the work of the other, and have his own go on at the same time.

Mr. Covey was at the house, about one hundred yards from the treading-yard where we were fanning. On hearing the fan stop, he left immediately, and came to the spot where we were. He hastily inquired what the matter was. Bill answered that I was sick, and there was no one to bring wheat to the fan. I had by this time crawled away under the side of the post and rail-fence by which the yard was enclosed, hoping to find relief by getting out of the sun. He then asked where I was. He was told by one of the hands. He came to the spot, and, after looking at me awhile, asked me what was the matter. I told him as well as I could, for I scarce had strength to speak. He then gave me a savage kick in the side, and told me to get up. I tried to do so, but fell back in the attempt. He gave me another kick, and again told me to rise. I again tried, and succeeded in gaining my feet; but, stooping to get the tub with which I was feeding the fan, I again staggered and fell. While down in this situation, Mr. Covey took up the hickory slat with which Hughes had been striking off the half-bushel measure, and with it gave me a heavy blow upon the head, making a large wound, and the blood ran freely; and with this again told me to get up. I made no effort to comply, having now made up my mind to let him do his worst. In a short time after receiving this blow, my head grew better. Mr. Covey had now left me to my fate. At this moment I resolved, for the first time, to go to my master, enter a complaint, and ask his protection. In order to do this, I must that afternoon walk seven miles; and this, under the circumstances, was truly a severe undertaking. I was exceedingly feeble; made so as much by the kicks and blows which I received, as by the severe fit of sickness to which I had been subjected. I, however, watched my chance, while Covey was looking in an opposite direction, and started for St. Michael's. I succeeded in getting a considerable distance on my way to the woods, when Covey discovered me, and called after me to come back, threatening what he would do if I did not come. I disregarded both his calls and his threats, and made my way to the woods as fast as my feeble state would allow; and thinking I might be overhauled by him if I kept the road, I walked through the woods, keeping far enough from the road to avoid detection, and near enough to prevent losing my way. I had not gone far before my little strength again failed me. I could go no farther. I fell down, and lay for a considerable time. The blood was yet oozing from the wound on my head. For a time I thought I should bleed to death; and think now that I should have done so, but that the blood so matted my hair as to stop the wound. After lying there about three quarters of an hour, I nerved myself up

again, and started on my way, through bogs and briers, barefooted and bareheaded, tearing my feet sometimes at nearly
every step; and after a journey of about seven miles, occupying
some five hours to perform it, I arrived at master's store. I then
presented an appearance enough to affect any but a heart of iron.
From the crown of my head to my feet, I was covered with blood.
My hair was all clotted with dust and blood; my shirt was stiff
with blood. My legs and feet were torn in sundry places with
briers and thorns, and were also covered with blood. I suppose
I looked like a man who had escaped a den of wild beasts, and
barely escaped them. In this state I appeared before my master,
humbly entreating him to interpose his authority for my protection. I told him all the circumstances as well as I could, and
it seemed, as I spoke, at times to affect him. He would then
walk the floor, and seek to justify Covey by saying he expected
I deserved it. He asked me what I wanted. I told him, to let me
get a new home; that as sure as I lived with Mr. Covey again, I
should live with but to die with him; that Covey would surely
kill me; he was in a fair way for it. Master Thomas ridiculed
the idea that there was any danger of Mr. Covey's killing me,
and said that he knew Mr. Covey; that he was a good man, and
that he could not think of taking me from him; that, should he
do so, he would lose the whole year's wages; that I belonged to
Mr. Covey for one year, and that I must go back to him, come
what might; and that I must not trouble him with any more
stories, or that he would himself *get hold of me*. After threatening
me thus, he gave me a very large dose of salts, telling me that
I might remain in St. Michael's that night, (it being quite late,)
but that I must be off back to Mr. Covey's early in the morning;
and that if I did not, he would *get hold of me*, which meant that
he would whip me. I remained all night, and, according to his
orders, I started off to Covey's in the morning, (Saturday morning,) wearied in body and broken in spirit. I got no supper that
night, or breakfast that morning. I reached Covey's about nine
o'clock; and just as I was getting over the fence that divided

Mrs. Kemp's fields from ours, out ran Covey with his cowskin, to give me another whipping. Before he could reach me, I succeeded in getting to the cornfield; and as the corn was very high, it afforded me the means of hiding. He seemed very angry, and searched for me a long time. My behavior was altogether unaccountable. He finally gave up the chase, thinking, I suppose, that I must come home for something to eat; he would give himself no further trouble in looking for me. I spent that day mostly in the woods, having the alternative before me,—to go home and be whipped to death, or stay in the woods and be starved to death. That night, I fell in with Sandy Jenkins, a slave with whom I was somewhat acquainted. Sandy had a free wife, who lived about four miles from Mr. Covey's; and it being Saturday, he was on his way to see her. I told him my circumstances, and he very kindly invited me to go home with him. I went home with him, and talked this whole matter over, and got his advice as to what course it was best for me to pursue. I found Sandy an old adviser. He told me, with great solemnity, I must go back to Covey; but that before I went, I must go with him into another part of the woods, where there was a certain *root*, which, if I would take some of it with me, carrying it *always on my right side*, would render it impossible for Mr. Covey, or any other white man, to whip me. He said he had carried it for years; and since he had done so, he had never received a blow, and never expected to while he carried it. I at first rejected the idea, that the simple carrying of a root in my pocket would have any such effect as he had said, and was not disposed to take it; but Sandy impressed the necessity with much earnestness, telling me it could do no harm, if it did no good. To please him, I at length took the root, and, according to his direction, carried it upon my right side. This was Sunday morning. I immediately started for home; and upon entering the yard gate, out came Mr. Covey on his way to meeting. He spoke to me very kindly, bade me drive the pigs from a lot near by, and passed on towards the church. Now, this singular conduct of Mr. Covey really made me begin to think that there was something in the *root* which Sandy had given me; and had it been on any other day than Sunday, I could have attributed the conduct to no other cause than the influence of that root; and as it was, I was half inclined to think the *root* to be something more than I at first had taken it to be. All went well till Monday morning. On this morning, the virtue of the *root* was fully tested. Long before daylight, I was called to go and rub, curry, and feed, the horses. I obeyed, and was glad to obey. But whilst thus engaged, whilst in the act of throwing down some blades from the loft, Mr. Covey entered the stable with a long rope; and just as I was half out of the loft, he caught hold of my legs, and was about tying me. As soon as I found what he was up to, I gave a sudden spring, and as I did so, he holding to my legs, I was brought sprawling on the stable floor. Mr. Covey seemed now to think he had me, and could do what he pleased; but at this moment— from whence came the spirit I don't know—I resolved to fight; and, suiting my action to the resolution, I seized Covey hard by the throat; and as I did so, I rose. He held on to me, and I to him. My resistance was so entirely unexpected, that Covey seemed taken all aback. He trembled like a leaf. This gave me assurance, and I held him uneasy, causing the blood to run where I touched him with the ends of my fingers. Mr. Covey soon called out to Hughes for help. Hughes came, and, while Covey held me, attempted to tie my right hand. While he was in the act of doing so, I watched my chance, and gave him a heavy kick close under the ribs. This kick fairly sickened Hughes, so that he left me in the hands of Mr. Covey. This kick had the effect of not only weakening Hughes, but Covey also. When he saw Hughes bending over with pain, his courage quailed. He asked me if I meant to persist in my resistance. I told him I did, come what might; that he had used me like a brute for six months, and that I was determined to be used so no longer.

With that, he strove to drag me to a stick that was lying just out of the stable door. He meant to knock me down. But just as he was leaning over to get the stick, I seized him with both hands by his collar, and brought him by a sudden snatch to the ground. By this time, Bill came. Covey called upon him for assistance. Bill wanted to know what he could do. Covey said, "Take hold of him, take hold of him!" Bill said his master hired him out to work, and not to help to whip me; so he left Covey and myself to fight our own battle out. We were at it for nearly two hours. Covey at length let me go, puffing and blowing at a great rate, saying that if I had not resisted, he would not have whipped me half so much. The truth was, that he had not whipped me at all. I considered him as getting entirely the worst end of the bargain; for he had drawn no blood from me, but I had from him. The whole six months afterwards, that I spent with Mr. Covey, he never laid the weight of his finger upon me in anger. He would occasionally say, he didn't want to get hold of me again. "No," thought I, "you need not; for you will come off worse than you did before."

This battle with Mr. Covey was the turning-point in my career as a slave. It rekindled the few expiring embers of freedom, and revived within me a sense of my own manhood. It recalled the departed self-confidence, and inspired me again with a determination to be free. The gratification afforded by the triumph was a full compensation for whatever else might follow, even death itself. He only can understand the deep satisfaction which I experienced, who has himself repelled by force the bloody arm of slavery. I felt as I never felt before. It was a glorious resurrection, from the tomb of slavery, to the heaven of freedom. My long-crushed spirit rose, cowardice departed, bold defiance took its place; and I now resolved that, however long I might remain a slave in form, the day had passed forever when I could be a slave in fact. I did not hesitate to let it be known of me, that the white man who expected to succeed in whipping, must also succeed in killing me.

From this time I was never again what might be called fairly whipped, though I remained a slave four years afterwards. I had several fights, but was never whipped.

It was for a long time a matter of surprise to me why Mr. Covey did not immediately have me taken by the constable to the whipping-post, and there regularly whipped for the crime of raising my hand against a white man in defence of myself. And the only explanation I can now think of does not entirely satisfy me; but such as it is, I will give it. Mr. Covey enjoyed the most unbounded reputation for being a first-rate overseer and negro-breaker. It was of considerable importance to him. That reputation was at stake; and had he sent me—a boy about sixteen years old—to the public whipping-post, his reputation would have been lost; so, to save his reputation, he suffered me to go unpunished.

My term of actual service to Mr. Edward Covey ended on Christmas day, 1833. The days between Christmas and New Year's day are allowed as holidays; and, accordingly, we were not required to perform any labor, more than to feed and take care of the stock. This time we regarded as our own, by the grace of our masters; and we therefore used or abused it nearly as we pleased. Those of us who had families at a distance, were generally allowed to spend the whole six days in their society. This time, however, was spent in various ways. The staid, sober, thinking and industrious ones of our number would employ themselves in making corn-brooms, mats, horse-collars, and baskets; and another class of us would spend the time in hunting opossums, hares, and coons. But by far the larger part engaged in such sports and merriments as playing ball, wrestling, running foot-races, fiddling, dancing, and drinking whisky; and this latter mode of spending the time was by far the most agreeable to the feelings of our masters. A slave who would work during the holidays was considered by our masters as scarcely deserving them. He was regarded as one who rejected the favor of his master. It was deemed a disgrace not to get drunk at Christmas;

and he was regarded as lazy indeed, who had not provided himself with the necessary means, during the year, to get whisky enough to last him through Christmas.

From what I know of the effect of these holidays upon the slave, I believe them to be among the most effective means in the hands of the slaveholder in keeping down the spirit of insurrection. Were the slaveholders at once to abandon this practice, I have not the slightest doubt it would lead to an immediate insurrection among the slaves. These holidays serve as conductors, or safety-valves, to carry off the rebellious spirit of enslaved humanity. But for these, the slave would be forced up to the wildest desperation; and woe betide the slaveholder, the day he ventures to remove or hinder the operation of those conductors! I warn him that, in such an event, a spirit will go forth in their midst, more to be dreaded than the most appalling earthquake.

The holidays are part and parcel of the gross fraud, wrong, and inhumanity of slavery. They are professedly a custom established by the benevolence of the slaveholders; but I undertake to say, it is the result of selfishness, and one of the grossest frauds committed upon the downtrodden slave. They do not give the slaves this time because they would not like to have their work during its continuance, but because they know it would be unsafe to deprive them of it. This will be seen by the fact, that the slaveholders like to have their slaves spend those days just in such a manner as to make them as glad of their ending as of their beginning. Their object seems to be, to disgust their slaves with freedom, by plunging them into the lowest depths of dissipation. For instance, the slaveholders not only like to see the slave drink of his own accord, but will adopt various plans to make him drunk. One plan is, to make bets on their slaves, as to who can drink the most whisky without getting drunk; and in this way they succeed in getting whole multitudes to drink to excess. Thus, when the slave asks for virtuous freedom, the cunning slaveholder, knowing his ignorance, cheats him with a dose of vicious dissipation, artfully labelled with the name of liberty. The most of us used to drink it down, and the result was just what might be supposed: many of us were led to think that there was little to choose between liberty and slavery. We felt, and very properly too, that we had almost as well be slaves to man as to rum. So, when the holidays ended, we staggered up from the filth of our wallowing, took a long breath, and marched to the field,—feeling, upon the whole, rather glad to go, from what our master had deceived us into a belief was freedom, back to the arms of slavery.

I have said that this mode of treatment is a part of the whole system of fraud and inhumanity of slavery. It is so. The mode here adopted to disgust the slave with freedom, by allowing him to see only the abuse of it, is carried out in other things. For instance, a slave loves molasses; he steals some. His master, in many cases, goes off to town, and buys a large quantity; he returns, takes his whip, and commands the slave to eat the molasses, until the poor fellow is made sick at the very mention of it. The same mode is sometimes adopted to make the slaves refrain from asking for more food than their regular allowance. A slave runs through his allowance, and applies for more. His master is enraged at him; but, not willing to send him off without food, gives him more than is necessary, and compels him to eat it within a given time. Then, if he complains that he cannot eat it, he is said to be satisfied neither full nor fasting, and is whipped for being hard to please! I have an abundance of such illustrations of the same principle, drawn from my own observation, but think the cases I have cited sufficient. The practice is a very common one.

On the first of January, 1834, I left Mr. Covey, and went to live with Mr. William Freeland, who lived about three miles from St. Michael's. I soon found Mr. Freeland a very different man from Mr. Covey. Though not rich, he was what would be called an educated southern gentleman. Mr. Covey, as I have shown, was a well-trained negro-breaker and slave-driver. The former (slaveholder though he was) seemed to possess some

regard for honor, some reverence for justice, and some respect
for humanity. The latter seemed totally insensible to all such
sentiments. Mr. Freeland had many of the faults peculiar to
slaveholders, such as being very passionate and fretful; but I
must do him the justice to say, that he was exceedingly free
from those degrading vices to which Mr. Covey was constantly
addicted. The one was open and frank, and we always knew
where to find him. The other was a most artful deceiver, and
could be understood only by such as were skilful enough to
detect his cunningly-devised frauds. Another advantage I gained
in my new master was, he made no pretensions to, or profession
of, religion; and this, in my opinion, was truly a great advantage.
I assert most unhesitatingly, that the religion of the south is a
mere covering for the most horrid crimes,—a justifier of the
most appalling barbarity,—a sanctifier of the most hateful
frauds,—and a dark shelter under, which the darkest, foulest,
grossest, and most infernal deeds of slaveholders find the strongest protection. Were I to be again reduced to the chains of
slavery, next to that enslavement, I should regard being the slave
of a religious master the greatest calamity that could befall me.
For of all slaveholders with whom I have ever met, religious
slaveholders are the worst. I have ever found them the meanest
and basest, the most cruel and cowardly, of all others. It was
my unhappy lot not only to belong to a religious slaveholder,
but to live in a community of such religionists. Very near
Mr. Freeland lived the Rev. Daniel Weeden, and in the same
neighborhood lived the Rev. Rigby Hopkins. These were members and ministers in the Reformed Methodist Church.
Mr. Weeden owned, among others, a woman slave, whose name
I have forgotten. This woman's back, for weeks, was kept literally
raw, made so by the lash of this merciless, *religious* wretch. He
used to hire hands. His maxim was, Behave well or behave ill,
it is the duty of a master occasionally to whip a slave, to remind
him of his master's authority. Such was his theory, and such his
practice.

Mr. Hopkins was even worse than Mr. Weeden. His chief boast was his ability to manage slaves. The peculiar feature of his government was that of whipping slaves in advance of deserving it. He always managed to have one or more of his slaves to whip every Monday morning. He did this to alarm their fears, and strike terror into those who escaped. His plan was to whip for the smallest offences, to prevent the commission of large ones. Mr. Hopkins could always find some excuse for whipping a slave. It would astonish one, unaccustomed to a slaveholding life, to see with what wonderful ease a slaveholder can find things, of which to make occasion to whip a slave. A mere look, word, or motion,—a mistake, accident, or want of power,—are all matters for which a slave may be whipped at any time. Does a slave look dissatisfied? It is said, he has the devil in him, and it must be whipped out. Does he speak loudly when spoken to by his master? Then he is getting high-minded, and should be taken down a button-hole lower. Does he forget to pull off his hat at the approach of a white person? Then he is wanting in reverence, and should be whipped for it. Does he ever venture to vindicate his conduct, when censured for it? Then he is guilty of impudence,—one of the greatest crimes of which a slave can be guilty. Does he ever venture to suggest a different mode of doing things from that pointed out by his master? He is indeed presumptuous, and getting above himself; and nothing less than a flogging will do for him. Does he, while ploughing, break a plough,—or, while hoeing, break a hoe? It is owing to his carelessness, and for it a slave must always be whipped. Mr. Hopkins could always find something of this sort to justify the use of the lash, and he seldom failed to embrace such opportunities. There was not a man in the whole county, with whom the slaves who had the getting their own home, would not prefer to live, rather than with this Rev. Mr. Hopkins. And yet there was not a man any where round, who made higher professions of religion, or was more active in revivals,—more attentive to the class, love-feast, prayer and preaching meetings, or more devotional in his family,—that prayed earlier, later, louder, and longer,—than this same reverend slave-driver, Rigby Hopkins.

But to return to Mr. Freeland, and to my experience while in his employment. He, like Mr. Covey, gave us enough to eat; but, unlike Mr. Covey, he also gave us sufficient time to take our meals. He worked us hard, but always between sunrise and sunset. He required a good deal of work to be done, but gave us good tools with which to work. His farm was large, but he employed hands enough to work it, and with ease, compared with many of his neighbors. My treatment, while in his employment, was heavenly, compared with what I experienced at the hands of Mr. Edward Covey.

Mr. Freeland was himself the owner of but two slaves. Their names were Henry Harris and John Harris. The rest of his hands he hired. These consisted of myself, Sandy Jenkins,[1] and Handy Caldwell. Henry and John were quite intelligent, and in a very little while after I went there, I succeeded in creating in them a strong desire to learn how to read. This desire soon sprang up in the others also. They very soon mustered up some old spelling-books, and nothing would do but that I must keep a Sabbath school. I agreed to do so, and accordingly devoted my Sundays to teaching these my loved fellow-slaves how to read. Neither of them knew his letters when I went there. Some of the slaves of the neighboring farms found what was going on, and also availed themselves of this little opportunity to learn to read. It was understood, among all who came, that there must be as little display about it as possible. It was necessary to keep our religious masters at St. Michael's unacquainted with the

---

1 This is the same man who gave me the roots to prevent my being whipped by Mr. Covey. He was "a clever soul." We used frequently to talk about the fight with Covey, and as often as we did so, he would claim my success as the result of the roots which he gave me. This superstition is very common among the more ignorant slaves. A slave seldom dies but that his death is attributed to trickery.

fact, that, instead of spending the Sabbath in wrestling, boxing, and drinking whisky, we were trying to learn how to read the will of God; for they had much rather see us engaged in those degrading sports, than to see us behaving like intellectual, moral, and accountable beings. My blood boils as I think of the bloody manner in which Messrs. Wright Fairbanks and Garrison West, both class-leaders, in connection with many others, rushed in upon us with sticks and stones, and broke up our virtuous little Sabbath school, at St. Michael's—all calling themselves Christians! humble followers of the Lord Jesus Christ! But I am again digressing.

I held my Sabbath school at the house of a free colored man, whose name I deem it imprudent to mention; for should it be known, it might embarrass him greatly, though the crime of holding the school was committed ten years ago. I had at one time over forty scholars, and those of the right sort, ardently desiring to learn. They were of all ages, though mostly men and women. I look back to those Sundays with an amount of pleasure not to be expressed. They were great days to my soul. The work of instructing my dear fellow-slaves was the sweetest engagement with which I was ever blessed. We loved each other, and to leave them at the close of the Sabbath was a severe cross indeed. When I think that these precious souls are to-day shut up in the prison-house of slavery, my feelings overcome me, and I am almost ready to ask, "Does a righteous God govern the universe? and for what does he hold the thunders in his right hand, if not to smite the oppressor, and deliver the spoiled out of the hand of the spoiler?" These dear souls came not to Sabbath school because it was popular to do so, nor did I teach them because it was reputable to be thus engaged. Every moment they spent in that school, they were liable to be taken up, and given thirty-nine lashes. They came because they wished to learn. Their minds had been starved by their cruel masters. They had been shut up in mental darkness. I taught them, because it was the delight of my soul to be doing something that looked like bettering the condition of my race. I kept up my school nearly the whole year I lived with Mr. Freeland; and, beside my Sabbath school, I devoted three evenings in the week, during the winter, to teaching the slaves at home. And I have the happiness to know, that several of those who came to Sabbath school learned how to read; and that one, at least, is now free through my agency.

The year passed off smoothly. It seemed only about half as long as the year which preceded it. I went through it without receiving a single blow. I will give Mr. Freeland the credit of being the best master I ever had, *till I became my own master*. For the ease with which I passed the year, I was, however, somewhat indebted to the society of my fellow-slaves. They were noble souls; they not only possessed loving hearts, but brave ones. We were linked and interlinked with each other. I loved them with a love stronger than any thing I have experienced since. It is sometimes said that we slaves do not love and confide in each other. In answer to this assertion, I can say, I never loved any or confided in any people more than my fellow-slaves, and especially those with whom I lived at Mr. Freeland's. I believe we would have died for each other. We never undertook to do any thing, of any importance, without a mutual consultation. We never moved separately. We were one; and as much so by our tempers and dispositions, as by the mutual hardships to which we were necessarily subjected by our condition as slaves.

At the close of the year 1834, Mr. Freeland again hired me of my master, for the year 1835. But, by this time, I began to want *to live upon free land* as well as *with Freeland*; and I was no longer content, therefore, to live with him or any other slave-holder. I began, with the commencement of the year, to prepare myself for a final struggle, which should decide my fate one way or the other. My tendency was upward. I was fast approaching manhood, and year after year had passed, and I was still a slave. These thoughts roused me—I must do something. I therefore resolved that 1835 should not pass without witnessing an attempt, on my part, to secure my liberty. But I was not willing to cherish this determination alone. My fellow-slaves were dear to me. I was anxious to have them participate with me in this, my life-giving determination. I therefore, though with great prudence, commenced early to ascertain their views and feelings in regard to their condition, and to imbue their minds with thoughts of freedom. I bent myself to devising ways and means for our escape, and meanwhile strove, on all fitting occasions, to impress them with the gross fraud and inhumanity of slavery. I went first to Henry, next to John, then to the others. I found, in them all, warm hearts and noble spirits. They were ready to hear, and ready to act when a feasible plan should be proposed. This was what I wanted. I talked to them of our want of man-hood, if we submitted to our enslavement without at least one noble effort to be free. We met often, and consulted frequently, and told our hopes and fears, recounted the difficulties, real and imagined, which we should be called on to meet. At times we were almost disposed to give up, and try to content ourselves with our wretched lot; at others, we were firm and unbending in our determination to go. Whenever we suggested any plan, there was shrinking—the odds were fearful. Our path was beset with the greatest obstacles; and if we succeeded in gaining the end of it, our right to be free was yet questionable—we were yet liable to be returned to bondage. We could see no spot, this side of the ocean, where we could be free. We knew nothing about Canada. Our knowledge of the north did not extend farther than New York; and to go there, and be forever harassed with the frightful liability of being returned to slavery—with the certainty of being treated tenfold worse than before—the thought was truly a horrible one, and one which it was not easy to overcome. The case sometimes stood thus: At every gate through which we were to pass, we saw a watchman—at every ferry a guard—on every bridge a sentinel—and in every wood a patrol. We were hemmed in upon every side. Here were the difficulties, real or imagined—the good to be sought, and the evil to be shunned. On the one hand, there stood slavery, a stern reality, glaring frightfully upon us,—its robes already crimsoned with the blood of millions, and even now feasting itself greedily upon our own flesh. On the other hand, away back in the dim distance, under the flickering light of the north star, behind some craggy hill or snow-covered mountain, stood a doubtful freedom—half frozen—beckoning us to come and share its hospitality. This in itself was sometimes enough to stagger us; but when we permitted ourselves to survey the road, we were frequently appalled. Upon either side we saw grim death, assuming the most horrid shapes. Now it was starvation, causing us to eat our own flesh;—now we were contending with the waves, and were drowned;—now we were overtaken, and torn to pieces by the fangs of the terrible bloodhound. We were stung by scorpions, chased by wild beasts, bitten by snakes, and finally, after having nearly reached the desired spot,—after swimming rivers, encountering wild beasts, sleeping in the woods, suffering hunger and nakedness,—we were overtaken by our pursuers, and, in our resistance, we were shot dead upon the spot! I say, this picture sometimes appalled us, and made us

> "rather bear those ills we had,
> Than fly to others, that we knew not of."

In coming to a fixed determination to run away, we did more than Patrick Henry, when he resolved upon liberty or death. With us it was a doubtful liberty at most, and almost certain death if we failed. For my part, I should prefer death to hopeless bondage.

Sandy, one of our number, gave up the notion, but still encouraged us. Our company then consisted of Henry Harris, John Harris, Henry Bailey, Charles Roberts, and myself. Henry Bailey was my uncle, and belonged to my master. Charles married my aunt: he belonged to my master's father-in-law, Mr. William Hamilton.

The plan we finally concluded upon was, to get a large canoe belonging to Mr. Hamilton, and upon the Saturday night previous to Easter holidays, paddle directly up the Chesapeake Bay. On our arrival at the head of the bay, a distance of seventy or eighty miles from where we lived, it was our purpose to turn our canoe adrift, and follow the guidance of the north star till we got beyond the limits of Maryland. Our reason for taking the water route was, that we were less liable to be suspected as runaways; we hoped to be regarded as fishermen; whereas, if we should take the land route, we should be subjected to interruptions of almost every kind. Any one having a white face, and being so disposed, could stop us, and subject us to examination.

The week before our intended start, I wrote several protections, one for each of us. As well as I can remember, they were in the following words, to wit:—

"THIS is to certify that I, the undersigned, have given the bearer, my servant, full liberty to go to Baltimore, and spend the Easter holidays. Written with mine own hand, &c., 1835.

"WILLIAM HAMILTON,

"Near St. Michael's, in Talbot county, Maryland."

We were not going to Baltimore; but, in going up the bay, we went toward Baltimore, and these protections were only intended to protect us while on the bay.

As the time drew near for our departure, our anxiety became more and more intense. It was truly a matter of life and death with us. The strength of our determination was about to be fully tested. At this time, I was very active in explaining every difficulty, removing every doubt, dispelling every fear, and inspiring all with the firmness indispensable to success in our undertaking; assuring them that half was gained the instant we made the move; we had talked long enough; we were now ready to move; if not now, we never should be; and if we did not intend to move now, we had as well fold our arms, sit down, and acknowledge ourselves fit only to be slaves. This, none of us were prepared to acknowledge. Every man stood firm; and at our last meeting, we pledged ourselves afresh, in the most solemn manner, that, at the time appointed, we would certainly start in pursuit of freedom. This was in the middle of the week, at the end of which we were to be off. We went, as usual, to our several fields of labor, but with bosoms highly agitated with thoughts of our truly hazardous undertaking. We tried to conceal our feelings as much as possible; and I think we succeeded very well.

After a painful waiting, the Saturday morning, whose night was to witness our departure, came. I hailed it with joy, bring what of sadness it might. Friday night was a sleepless one for me. I probably felt more anxious than the rest, because I was, by common consent, at the head of the whole affair. The responsibility of success or failure lay heavily upon me. The glory of the one, and the confusion of the other, were alike mine. The first two hours of that morning were such as I never experienced before, and hope never to again. Early in the morning, we went, as usual, to the field. We were spreading manure; and all at once, while thus engaged, I was overwhelmed with an indescribable feeling, in the fulness of which I turned to Sandy, who was near by, and said, "We are betrayed!" "Well," said he, "that thought has this moment struck me." We said no more. I was never more certain of any thing.

The horn was blown as usual, and we went up from the field to the house for breakfast. I went for the form, more than for want of any thing to eat that morning. Just as I got to the house, in looking out at the lane gate, I saw four white men, with two colored men. The white men were on horseback, and the colored ones were walking behind, as if tied. I watched them a few moments till they got up to our lane gate. Here they halted, and tied the colored men to the gate-post. I was not yet certain as to what the matter was. In a few moments, in rode Mr. Hamilton, with a speed betokening great excitement. He came to the door, and inquired if Master William was in. He was told he was at the barn. Mr. Hamilton, without dismounting, rode up to the barn with extraordinary speed. In a few moments, he and Mr. Freeland returned to the house. By this time, the three constables rode up, and in great haste dismounted, tied their horses, and met Master William and Mr. Hamilton returning from the barn; and after talking awhile, they all walked up to the kitchen door. There was no one in the kitchen but myself and John. Henry and Sandy were up at the barn. Mr. Freeland put his head in at the door, and called me by name, saying, there were some gentlemen at the door who wished to see me. I stepped to the door, and inquired what they wanted. They at once seized me, and, without giving me any satisfaction, tied me—lashing my hands closely together. I insisted upon knowing what the matter was. They at length said, that they had learned I had been in a "scrape," and that I was to be examined before my master; and if their information proved false, I should not be hurt.

In a few moments, they succeeded in tying John. They then turned to Henry, who had by this time returned, and commanded him to cross his hands. "I won't!" said Henry, in a firm tone, indicating his readiness to meet the consequences of his refusal. "Won't you?" said Tom Graham, the constable. "No, I won't!" said Henry, in a still stronger tone. With this, two of the constables pulled out their shining pistols, and swore, by their Creator, that they would make him cross his hands or kill him. Each cocked his pistol, and, with fingers on the trigger, walked up to Henry, saying, at the same time, if he did not cross his hands, they would blow his damned heart out. "Shoot me, shoot me!" said Henry; "you can't kill me but once. Shoot, shoot,—and be damned! *I wont be tied!*" This he said in a tone of loud defiance;

and at the same time, with a motion as quick as lightning, he with one single stroke dashed the pistols from the hand of each constable. As he did this, all hands fell upon him, and, after beating him some time, they finally overpowered him, and got him tied.

During the scuffle, I managed, I know not how, to get my pass out, and, without being discovered, put it into the fire. We were all now tied; and just as we were to leave for Easton jail, Betsy Freeland, mother of William Freeland, came to the door with her hands full of biscuits, and divided them between Henry and John. She then delivered herself of a speech, to the following effect:—addressing herself to me, she said, "*You devil! You yellow devil!* it was you that put it into the heads of Henry and John to run away. But for you, you long-legged mulatto devil! Henry nor John would never have thought of such a thing." I made no reply, and was immediately hurried off towards St. Michael's. Just a moment previous to the scuffle with Henry, Mr. Hamilton suggested the propriety of making a search for the protections which he had understood Frederick had written for himself and the rest. But, just at the moment he was about carrying his proposal into effect, his aid was needed in helping to tie Henry; and the excitement attending the scuffle caused them either to forget, or to deem it unsafe, under the circumstances, to search. So we were not yet convicted of the intention to run away.

When we got about half way to St. Michael's, while the constables having us in charge were looking ahead, Henry inquired of me what he should do with his pass. I told him to eat it with his biscuit, and own nothing; and we passed the word around, "*Own nothing;*" and "*Own nothing!*" said we all. Our confidence in each other was unshaken. We were resolved to succeed or fail together, after the calamity had befallen us as much as before. We were now prepared for any thing. We were to be dragged that morning fifteen miles behind horses, and then to be placed in the Easton jail. When we reached St. Michael's, we underwent a sort of examination. We all denied that we ever intended to run away. We did this more to bring out the evidence against us, than from any hope of getting clear of being sold; for, as I have said, we were ready for that. The fact was, we cared but little where we went, so we went together. Our greatest concern was about separation. We dreaded that more than any thing this side of death. We found the evidence against us to be the testimony of one person; our master would not tell who it was; but we came to a unanimous decision among ourselves as to who their informant was. We were sent off to the jail at Easton. When we got there, we were delivered up to the sheriff, Mr. Joseph Graham, and by him placed in jail. Henry, John, and myself, were placed in one room together—Charles, and Henry Bailey, in another. Their object in separating us was to hinder concert.

We had been in jail scarcely twenty minutes, when a swarm of slave traders, and agents for slave traders, flocked into jail to look at us, and to ascertain if we were for sale. Such a set of beings I never saw before! I felt myself surrounded by so many fiends from perdition. A band of pirates never looked more like their father, the devil. They laughed and grinned over us, saying, "Ah, my boys! we have got you, haven't we?" And after taunting us in various ways, they one by one went into an examination of us, with intent to ascertain our value. They would impudently ask us if we would not like to have them for our masters. We would make them no answer, and leave them to find out as best they could. Then they would curse and swear at us, telling us that they could take the devil out of us in a very little while, if we were only in their hands.

While in jail, we found ourselves in much more comfortable quarters than we expected when we went there. We did not get much to eat, nor that which was very good; but we had a good clean room, from the windows of which we could see what was going on in the street, which was very much better than though we had been placed in one of the dark, damp cells. Upon the whole, we got along very well, so far as the jail and its keeper were concerned. Immediately after the holidays were over, contrary to all our expectations, Mr. Hamilton and Mr. Freeland came up to Easton, and took Charles, the two Henrys, and John, out of jail, and carried them home, leaving me alone. I regarded this separation as a final one. It caused me more pain than any thing else in the whole transaction. I was ready for any thing rather than separation. I supposed that they had consulted together, and had decided that, as I was the whole cause of the intention of the others to run away, it was hard to make the innocent suffer with the guilty; and that they had, therefore, concluded to take the others home, and sell me, as a warning to the others that remained. It is due to the noble Henry to say, he seemed almost as reluctant at leaving the prison as at leaving home to come to the prison. But we knew we should, in all probability, be separated, if we were sold; and since he was in their hands, he concluded to go peaceably home.

I was now left to my fate. I was all alone, and within the walls of a stone prison. But a few days before, and I was full of hope. I expected to have been safe in a land of freedom; but now I was covered with gloom, sunk down to the utmost despair. I thought the possibility of freedom was gone. I was kept in this way about one week, at the end of which, Captain Auld, my master, to my surprise and utter astonishment, came up, and took me out, with the intention of sending me, with a gentleman of his acquaintance, into Alabama. But, from some cause or other, he did not send me to Alabama, but concluded to send me back to Baltimore, to live again with his brother Hugh, and to learn a trade.

Thus, after an absence of three years and one month, I was once more permitted to return to my old home at Baltimore. My master sent me away, because there existed against me a very great prejudice in the community, and he feared I might be killed.

In a few weeks after I went to Baltimore, Master Hugh hired me to Mr. William Gardner, an extensive ship-builder, on Fell's Point. I was put there to learn how to calk. It, however, proved a very unfavorable place for the accomplishment of this object. Mr. Gardner was engaged that spring in building two large man-of-war brigs, professedly for the Mexican government. The vessels were to be launched in the July of that year, and in failure thereof, Mr. Gardner was to lose a considerable sum; so that when I entered, all was hurry. There was no time to learn any thing. Every man had to do that which he knew how to do. In entering the ship-yard, my orders from Mr. Gardner were, to do whatever the carpenters commanded me to do. This was placing me at the beck and call of about seventy-five men. I was to regard all these as masters. Their word was to be my law. My situation was a most trying one. At times I needed a dozen pair of hands. I was called a dozen ways in the space of a single minute. Three or four voices would strike my ear at the same moment. It was—"Fred., come help me to cant this timber here."—"Fred., come carry this timber yonder."—"Fred., bring that roller here."—"Fred., go get a fresh can of water."—"Fred., come help saw off the end of this timber."—"Fred., go quick, and get the crowbar."—"Fred., hold on the end of this fall."—"Fred., go to the blacksmith's shop, and get a new punch."—"Hurra, Fred.! run and bring me a cold chisel."—"I say, Fred., bear a hand, and get up a fire as quick as lightning under that steam-box."—"Halloo, nigger! come, turn this grind-stone."—"Come, come! move, move! and *bowse* this timber forward."—"I say, darky, blast your eyes, why don't you heat up some pitch?"—"Halloo! halloo! halloo!" (Three voices at the same time.) "Come here!—Go there!—Hold on where you are! Damn you, if you move, I'll knock your brains out!"

This was my school for eight months; and I might have remained there longer, but for a most horrid fight I had with four of the white apprentices, in which my left eye was nearly knocked out, and I was horribly mangled in other respects. The facts in the case were these: Until a very little while after I went there, white and black ship-carpenters worked side by side, and no one seemed to see any impropriety in it. All hands seemed to be very well satisfied. Many of the black carpenters were freemen. Things seemed to be going on very well. All at once, the white carpenters knocked off, and said they would not work with free colored workmen. Their reason for this, as alleged, was, that if free colored carpenters were encouraged, they would soon take the trade into their own hands, and poor white men would be thrown out of employment. They therefore felt called upon at once to put a stop to it. And, taking advantage of Mr. Gardner's necessities, they broke off, swearing they would work no longer, unless he would discharge his black carpenters. Now, though this did not extend to me in form, it did reach me in fact. My fellow-apprentices very soon began to feel it degrading to them to work with me. They began to put on airs, and talk about the "niggers" taking the country, saying we all ought to be killed; and, being encouraged by the journeymen, they commenced making my condition as hard as they could, by hectoring me around, and sometimes striking me. I, of course, kept the vow I made after the fight with Mr. Covey, and struck back again, regardless of consequences; and while I kept them from combining, I succeeded very well; for I could whip the whole of them, taking them separately. They, however, at length combined, and came upon me, armed with sticks, stones, and heavy handspikes. One came in front with a half brick. There was one at each side of me, and one behind me. While I was attending to those in front, and on either side, the one behind ran up with the handspike, and struck me a heavy blow upon the head. It stunned me. I fell, and with this they all ran upon me, and fell to beating me with their fists. I let them lay on for a while, gathering strength. In an instant, I gave a sudden surge, and rose to my hands and knees. Just as I did that, one of their number gave me, with his heavy boot, a powerful kick in the left eye. My eyeball seemed to have burst. When they saw my eye closed, and badly swollen, they left me. With this I seized the handspike, and for a time pursued them. But here the carpenters interfered, and I thought I might as well give it up. It was impossible to stand my hand against so many. All this took place in sight of not less than fifty white ship-carpenters, and not one interposed a friendly word; but some cried, "Kill the damned nigger! Kill him! kill him! He struck a white person." I found my only chance for life was in flight. I succeeded in getting away without an additional blow, and barely so; for to strike a white man is death by Lynch law,—and that was the law in Mr. Gardner's ship-yard; nor is there much of any other out of Mr. Gardner's ship-yard.

I went directly home, and told the story of my wrongs to Master Hugh; and I am happy to say of him, irreligious as he was, his conduct was heavenly, compared with that of his brother Thomas under similar circumstances. He listened attentively to my narration of the circumstances leading to the savage outrage, and gave many proofs of his strong indignation at it. The heart of my once overkind mistress was again melted into pity. My puffed-out eye and blood-covered face moved her to tears. She took a chair by me, washed the blood from my face, and, with a mother's tenderness, bound up my head, covering the wounded eye with a lean piece of fresh beef. It was almost compensation for my suffering to witness, once more, a manifestation of kindness from this, my once affectionate old mistress. Master Hugh was very much enraged. He gave expression to his feelings by pouring out curses upon the heads of those who did the deed. As soon as I got a little the better of my bruises, he took me with him to Esquire Watson's, on Bond Street, to see what could be done about the matter. Mr. Watson inquired who saw the assault committed. Master Hugh told him it was done in Mr. Gardner's ship-yard, at mid-day, where there were a large company of men at work. "As to that," he said, "the deed was done, and there was no question as to who did it." His answer was, he could do nothing in the case, unless some white man would come forward and testify. He could issue no warrant on my word. If I had been killed in the presence of a thousand colored people, their testimony combined would have been insufficient to have arrested one of the murderers. Master Hugh, for once, was compelled to say this state of things was too bad. Of course, it was impossible to get any white man to volunteer his testimony in my behalf, and against the white young men. Even those who may have sympathized with me were not prepared to do this. It required a degree of courage unknown to them to do so; for just at that time, the slightest manifestation of humanity toward a colored person was denounced as abolitionism, and that name subjected its bearer to frightful liabilities. The watchwords of the bloody-minded in that region, and in those days, were, "Damn the abolitionists!" and "Damn the niggers!" There was nothing done, and probably nothing would have been done if I had been killed. Such was, and such remains, the state of things in the Christian city of Baltimore.

Master Hugh, finding he could get no redress, refused to let me go back again to Mr. Gardner. He kept me himself, and his wife dressed my wound till I was again restored to health. He then took me into the shipyard of which he was foreman, in the employment of Mr. Walter Price. There I was immediately set to calking, and very soon learned the art of using my mallet and irons. In the course of one year from the time I left Mr. Gardner's, I was able to command the highest wages given to the most experienced calkers. I was now of some importance to my master. I was bringing him from six to seven dollars per week. I sometimes brought him nine dollars per week: my wages were a dollar and a half a day. After learning how to calk, I sought my own employment, made my own contracts, and collected the money which I earned. My pathway became much more smooth than before; my condition was now much more comfortable. When I could get no calking to do, I did nothing. During these leisure times, those old notions about freedom would steal over me again. When in Mr. Gardner's employment, I was kept in such a perpetual whirl of excitement, I could think of nothing, scarcely, but my life; and in thinking of my life, I almost forgot my liberty. I have observed this in my experience of slavery,— that whenever my condition was improved, instead of its increasing my contentment, it only increased my desire to be free, and set me to thinking of plans to gain my freedom. I have found that, to make a contented slave, it is necessary to make a thoughtless one. It is necessary to darken his moral and mental vision, and, as far as possible, to annihilate the power of reason. He must be able to detect no inconsistencies in slavery; he must be made to feel that slavery is right; and he can be brought to that only when he ceases to be a man.

I was now getting, as I have said, one dollar and fifty cents per day. I contracted for it; I earned it; it was paid to me; it was rightfully my own; yet, upon each returning Saturday night, I was compelled to deliver every cent of that money to Master Hugh. And why? Not because he earned it,—not because he had any hand in earning it,—not because I owed it to him,—nor because he possessed the slightest shadow of a right to it; but solely because he had the power to compel me to give it up. The right of the grim-visaged pirate upon the high seas is exactly the same.

Chapter XI

I now come to that part of my life during which I planned, and finally succeeded in making, my escape from slavery. But before narrating any of the peculiar circumstances, I deem it proper to make known my intention not to state all the facts connected with the transaction. My reasons for pursuing this course may be understood from the following: First, were I to give a minute statement of all the facts, it is not only possible, but quite probable, that others would thereby be involved in the most embarrassing difficulties. Secondly, such a statement would most undoubtedly induce greater vigilance on the part of slaveholders than has existed heretofore among them; which would, of course, be the means of guarding a door whereby some dear brother bondman might escape his galling chains. I deeply regret the necessity that impels me to suppress any thing of importance connected with my experience in slavery. It would afford me great pleasure indeed, as well as materially add to the interest of my narrative, were I at liberty to gratify a curiosity, which I know exists in the minds of many, by an accurate statement of all the facts pertaining to my most fortunate escape. But I must deprive myself of this pleasure, and the curious of the gratification which such a statement would afford. I would allow myself to suffer under the greatest imputations which evil-minded men might suggest, rather than exculpate myself, and thereby run the hazard of closing the slightest avenue by which a brother slave might clear himself of the chains and fetters of slavery.

I have never approved of the very public manner in which some of our western friends have conducted what they call the *underground railroad*, but which, I think, by their open declarations, has been made most emphatically the *upperground railroad*. I honor those good men and women for their noble daring, and applaud them for willingly subjecting themselves to bloody persecution, by openly avowing their participation in the escape of slaves. I, however, can see very little good resulting from such a course, either to themselves or the slaves escaping; while, upon the other hand, I see and feel assured that those open declarations are a positive evil to the slaves remaining, who are seeking to escape. They do nothing towards enlightening the slave, whilst they do much towards enlightening the master. They stimulate him to greater watchfulness, and enhance his power to capture his slave. We owe something to the slaves south of the line as well as to those north of it; and in aiding the latter on their way to freedom, we should be careful to do nothing which would be likely to hinder the former from escaping from slavery. I would keep the merciless slaveholder profoundly ignorant of the means of flight adopted by the slave. I would leave him to imagine himself surrounded by myriads of invisible tormentors, ever ready to snatch from his infernal grasp his trembling prey. Let him be left to feel his way in the dark; let darkness commensurate with his crime hover over him; and let him feel that at every step he takes, in pursuit of the flying bondman, he is running the frightful risk of having his hot brains dashed out by an invisible agency. Let us render the tyrant no aid; let us not hold the light by which he can trace the footprints of our flying brother. But enough of this. I will now proceed to the statement of those facts, connected with my escape, for which I am alone responsible, and for which no one can be made to suffer but myself.

In the early part of the year 1838, I became quite restless. I could see no reason why I should, at the end of each week, pour the reward of my toil into the purse of my master. When

I carried to him my weekly wages, he would, after counting the money, look me in the face with a robber-like fierceness, and ask, "Is this all?" He was satisfied with nothing less than the last cent. He would, however, when I made him six dollars, sometimes give me six cents, to encourage me. It had the opposite effect. I regarded it as a sort of admission of my right to the whole. The fact that he gave me any part of my wages was proof, to my mind, that he believed me entitled to the whole of them. I always felt worse for having received any thing; for I feared that the giving me a few cents would ease his conscience, and make him feel himself to be a pretty honorable sort of robber. My discontent grew upon me. I was ever on the look-out for means of escape; and, finding no direct means, I determined to try to hire my time, with a view of getting money with which to make my escape. In the spring of 1838, when Master Thomas came to Baltimore to purchase his spring goods, I got an opportunity, and applied to him to allow me to hire my time. He unhesitatingly refused my request, and told me this was another stratagem by which to escape. He told me I could go nowhere but that he could get me; and that, in the event of my running away, he should spare no pains in his efforts to catch me. He exhorted me to content myself, and be obedient. He told me, if I would be happy, I must lay out no plans for the future. He said, if I behaved myself properly, he would take care of me. Indeed, he advised me to complete thoughtlessness of the future, and taught me to depend solely upon him for happiness. He seemed to see fully the pressing necessity of setting aside my intellectual nature, in order to contentment in slavery. But in spite of him, and even in spite of myself, I continued to think, and to think about the injustice of my enslavement, and the means of escape.

About two months after this, I applied to Master Hugh for the privilege of hiring my time. He was not acquainted with the fact that I had applied to Master Thomas, and had been refused. He too, at first, seemed disposed to refuse; but, after some reflection, he granted me the privilege, and proposed the following terms: I was to be allowed all my time, make all contracts with those for whom I worked, and find my own employment; and, in return for this liberty, I was to pay him three dollars at the end of each week; find myself in calking tools, and in board and clothing. My board was two dollars and a half per week. This, with the wear and tear of clothing and calking tools, made my regular expenses about six dollars per week. This amount I was compelled to make up, or relinquish the privilege of hiring my time. Rain or shine, work or no work, at the end of each week the money must be forthcoming, or I must give up my privilege. This arrangement, it will be perceived, was decidedly in my master's favor. It relieved him of all need of looking after me. His money was sure. He received all the benefits of slaveholding without its evils; while I endured all the evils of a slave, and suffered all the care and anxiety of a freeman. I found it a hard bargain. But, hard as it was, I thought it better than the old mode of getting along. It was a step towards freedom to be allowed to bear the responsibilities of a freeman, and I was determined to hold on upon it. I bent myself to the work of making money. I was ready to work at night as well as day, and by the most untiring perseverance and industry, I made enough to meet my expenses, and lay up a little money every week. I went on thus from May till August. Master Hugh then refused to allow me to hire my time longer. The ground for his refusal was a failure on my part, one Saturday night, to pay him for my week's time. This failure was occasioned by my attending a camp meeting about ten miles from Baltimore. During the week, I had entered into an engagement with a number of young friends to start from Baltimore to the camp ground early Saturday evening; and being detained by my employer, I was unable to get down to Master Hugh's without disappointing the company. I knew that Master Hugh was in no special need of the money that night. I therefore decided to go to camp meeting, and upon my return pay him the three dollars. I staid at the camp meeting one day longer than I intended when I left. But as soon as

I returned, I called upon him to pay him what he considered his due. I found him very angry; he could scarce restrain his wrath. He said he had a great mind to give me a severe whipping. He wished to know how I dared go out of the city without asking his permission. I told him I hired my time, and while I paid him the price which he asked for it, I did not know that I was bound to ask him when and where I should go. This reply troubled him; and, after reflecting a few moments, he turned to me, and said I should hire my time no longer; that the next thing he should know of, I would be running away. Upon the same plea, he told me to bring my tools and clothing home forthwith. I did so; but instead of seeking work, as I had been accustomed to do previously to hiring my time, I spent the whole week without the performance of a single stroke of work. I did this in retaliation. Saturday night, he called upon me as usual for my week's wages. I told him I had no wages; I had done no work that week. Here we were upon the point of coming to blows. He raved, and swore his determination to get hold of me. I did not allow myself a single word; but was resolved, if he laid the weight of his hand upon me, it should be blow for blow. He did not strike me, but told me that he would find me in constant employment in future. I thought the matter over during the next day, Sunday, and finally resolved upon the third day of September, as the day upon which I would make a second attempt to secure my freedom. I now had three weeks during which to prepare for my journey. Early on Monday morning, before Master Hugh had time to make any engagement for me, I went out and got employment of Mr. Butler, at his ship-yard near the draw-bridge, upon what is called the City Block, thus making it unnecessary for him to seek employment for me. At the end of the week, I brought him between eight and nine dollars. He seemed very well pleased, and asked me why I did not do the same the week before. He little knew what my plans were. My object in working steadily was to remove any suspicion he might entertain of my intent to run away; and in this I succeeded admirably. I suppose he thought I was never better satisfied with my condition than at the very time during which I was planning my escape. The second week passed, and again I carried him my full wages; and so well pleased was he, that he gave me twenty-five cents, (quite a large sum for a slaveholder to give a slave,) and bade me to make a good use of it. I told him I would.

Things went on without very smoothly indeed, but within there was trouble. It is impossible for me to describe my feelings as the time of my contemplated start drew near. I had a number of warm-hearted friends in Baltimore,—friends that I loved almost as I did my life,—and the thought of being separated from them forever was painful beyond expression. It is my opinion that thousands would escape from slavery, who now remain, but for the strong cords of affection that bind them to their friends. The thought of leaving my friends was decidedly the most painful thought with which I had to contend. The love of them was my tender point, and shook my decision more than all things else. Besides the pain of separation, the dread and apprehension of a failure exceeded what I had experienced at my first attempt. The appalling defeat I then sustained returned to torment me. I felt assured that, if I failed in this attempt, my case would be a hopeless one—it would seal my fate as a slave forever. I could not hope to get off with any thing less than the severest punishment, and being placed beyond the means of escape. It required no very vivid imagination to depict the most frightful scenes through which I should have to pass, in case I failed. The wretchedness of slavery, and the blessedness of freedom, were perpetually before me. It was life and death with me. But I remained firm, and, according to my resolution, on the third day of September, 1838, I left my chains, and succeeded in reaching New York without the slightest interruption of any kind. How I did so,—what means I adopted,—what direction

I travelled, and by what mode of conveyance,—I must leave unexplained, for the reasons before mentioned.

I have been frequently asked how I felt when I found myself in a free State. I have never been able to answer the question with any satisfaction to myself. It was a moment of the highest excitement I ever experienced. I suppose I felt as one may imagine the unarmed mariner to feel when he is rescued by a friendly man-of-war from the pursuit of a pirate. In writing to a dear friend, immediately after my arrival at New York, I said I felt like one who had escaped a den of hungry lions. This state of mind, however, very soon subsided; and I was again seized with a feeling of great insecurity and loneliness. I was yet liable to be taken back, and subjected to all the tortures of slavery. This in itself was enough to damp the ardor of my enthusiasm. But the loneliness overcame me. There I was in the midst of thousands, and yet a perfect stranger; without home and without friends, in the midst of thousands of my own brethren—children of a common Father, and yet I dared not to unfold to any one of them my sad condition. I was afraid to speak to any one for fear of speaking to the wrong one, and thereby falling into the hands of money-loving kidnappers, whose business it was to lie in wait for the panting fugitive, as the ferocious beasts of the forest lie in wait for their prey. The motto which I adopted when I started from slavery was this—"Trust no man!" I saw in every white man an enemy, and in almost every colored man cause for distrust. It was a most painful situation; and, to understand it, one must needs experience it, or imagine himself in similar circumstances. Let him be a fugitive slave in a strange land—a land given up to be the hunting-ground for slaveholders—whose inhabitants are legalized kidnappers—where he is every moment subjected to the terrible liability of being seized upon by his fellow-men, as the hideous crocodile seizes upon his prey!—I say, let him place himself in my situation—without home or friends—without money or credit—wanting shelter, and no one to give it—wanting bread, and no money to buy it,—and at the same time let him feel that he is pursued by merciless men-hunters, and in total darkness as to what to do, where to go, or where to stay,—perfectly helpless both as to the means of defence and means of escape,—in the midst of plenty, yet suffering the terrible gnawings of hunger,—in the midst of houses, yet having no home,—among fellow-men, yet feeling as if in the midst of wild beasts, whose greediness to swallow up the trembling and half-famished fugitive is only equalled by that with which the monsters of the deep swallow up the helpless fish upon which they subsist,—I say, let him be placed in this most trying situation,—the situation in which I was placed,—then, and not till then, will he fully appreciate the hardships of, and know how to sympathize with, the toil-worn and whip-scarred fugitive slave.

Thank Heaven, I remained but a short time in this distressed situation. I was relieved from it by the humane hand of Mr. DAVID RUGGLES, whose vigilance, kindness, and perseverance, I shall never forget. I am glad of an opportunity to express, as far as words can, the love and gratitude I bear him. Mr. Ruggles is now afflicted with blindness, and is himself in need of the same kind offices which he was once so forward in the performance of toward others. I had been in New York but a few days, when Mr. Ruggles sought me out, and very kindly took me to his boarding-house at the corner of Church and Lespenard Streets. Mr. Ruggles was then very deeply engaged in the memorable *Darg* case, as well as attending to a number of other fugitive slaves, devising ways and means for their successful escape; and, though watched and hemmed in on almost every side, he seemed to be more than a match for his enemies.

Very soon after I went to Mr. Ruggles, he wished to know of me where I wanted to go; as he deemed it unsafe for me to remain in New York. I told him I was a calker, and should like to go where I could get work. I thought of going to Canada; but he decided against it, and in favor of my going to New

Bedford, thinking I should be able to get work there at my trade. At this time, Anna,[1] my intended wife, came on; for I wrote to her immediately after my arrival at New York, (notwithstanding my homeless, houseless, and helpless condition,) informing her of my successful flight, and wishing her to come on forthwith. In a few days after her arrival, Mr. Ruggles called in the Rev. J. W. C. Pennington, who, in the presence of Mr. Ruggles, Mrs. Michaels, and two or three others, performed the marriage ceremony, and gave us a certificate, of which the following is an exact copy:—

"THIS may certify, that I joined together in holy matrimony Frederick Johnson[2] and Anna Murray, as man and wife, in the presence of Mr. David Ruggles and Mrs. Michaels.

"JAMES W. C. PENNINGTON

"*New York, Sept.* 15, 1838"

Upon receiving this certificate, and a five-dollar bill from Mr. Ruggles, I shouldered one part of our baggage, and Anna took up the other, and we set out forthwith to take passage on board of the steamboat John W. Richmond for Newport, on our way to New Bedford. Mr. Ruggles gave me a letter to a Mr. Shaw in Newport, and told me, in case my money did not serve me to New Bedford, to stop in Newport and obtain further assistance; but upon our arrival at Newport, we were so anxious to get to a place of safety, that, notwithstanding we lacked the necessary money to pay our fare, we decided to take seats in the stage, and promise to pay when we got to New Bedford. We were encouraged to do this by two excellent gentlemen, residents of New Bedford, whose names I afterward ascertained

---

1 She was free.

2 I had changed my name from Frederick *Bailey* to that of *Johnson*.

to be Joseph Ricketson and William C. Taber. They seemed at once to understand our circumstances, and gave us such assurance of their friendliness as put us fully at ease in their presence. It was good indeed to meet with such friends, at such a time. Upon reaching New Bedford, we were directed to the house of Mr. Nathan Johnson, by whom we were kindly received, and hospitably provided for. Both Mr. and Mrs. Johnson took a deep and lively interest in our welfare. They proved themselves quite worthy of the name of abolitionists. When the stage-driver found us unable to pay our fare, he held on upon our baggage as security for the debt. I had but to mention the fact to Mr. Johnson, and he forthwith advanced the money.

We now began to feel a degree of safety, and to prepare ourselves for the duties and responsibilities of a life of freedom. On the morning after our arrival at New Bedford, while at the breakfast-table, the question arose as to what name I should be called by. The name given me by my mother was, "Frederick Augustus Washington Bailey." I, however, had dispensed with the two middle names long before I left Maryland, so that I was generally known by the name of "Frederick Bailey." I started from Baltimore bearing the name of "Stanley." When I got to New York, I again changed my name to "Frederick Johnson," and thought that would be the last change. But when I got to New Bedford, I found it necessary again to change my name. The reason of this necessity was, that there were so many Johnsons in New Bedford, it was already quite difficult to distinguish between them. I gave Mr. Johnson the privilege of choosing me a name, but told him he must not take from me the name of "Frederick." I must hold on to that, to preserve a sense of my identity. Mr. Johnson had just been reading the "Lady of the Lake," and at once suggested that my name be "Douglass." From that time until now I have been called "Frederick Douglass;" and as I am more widely known by that name than by either of the others, I shall continue to use it as my own.

I was quite disappointed at the general appearance of things in New Bedford. The impression which I had received respecting the character and condition of the people of the north, I found to be singularly erroneous. I had very strangely supposed, while in slavery, that few of the comforts, and scarcely any of the luxuries, of life were enjoyed at the north, compared with what were enjoyed by the slaveholders of the south. I probably came to this conclusion from the fact that northern people owned no slaves. I supposed that they were about upon a level with the non-slaveholding population of the south. I knew *they* were exceedingly poor, and I had been accustomed to regard their poverty as the necessary consequence of their being non-slaveholders. I had somehow imbibed the opinion that, in the absence of slaves, there could be no wealth, and very little refinement. And upon coming to the north, I expected to meet with a rough, hard-handed, and uncultivated population, living in the most Spartan-like simplicity, knowing nothing of the ease, luxury, pomp, and grandeur of southern slaveholders. Such being my conjectures, any one acquainted with the appearance of New Bedford may very readily infer how palpably I must have seen my mistake.

In the afternoon of the day when I reached New Bedford, I visited the wharves, to take a view of the shipping. Here I found myself surrounded with the strongest proofs of wealth. Lying at the wharves, and riding in the stream, I saw many ships of the finest model, in the best order, and of the largest size. Upon the right and left, I was walled in by granite warehouses of the widest dimensions, stowed to their utmost capacity with the necessaries and comforts of life. Added to this, almost every body seemed to be at work, but noiselessly so, compared with what I had been accustomed to in Baltimore. There were no loud songs heard from those engaged in loading and unloading ships. I heard no deep oaths or horrid curses on the laborer. I saw no whipping of men; but all seemed to go smoothly on. Every man appeared to understand his work, and went at it with a sober, yet cheerful earnestness, which betokened the deep interest which he felt in what he was doing, as well as a sense of his own dignity as a man. To me this looked exceedingly strange. From the wharves I strolled around and over the town, gazing with wonder and admiration at the splendid churches, beautiful dwellings, and finely-cultivated gardens; evincing an amount of wealth, comfort, taste, and refinement, such as I had never seen in any part of slaveholding Maryland.

Every thing looked clean, new, and beautiful. I saw few or no dilapidated houses, with poverty-stricken inmates; no half-naked children and barefooted women, such as I had been accustomed to see in Hillsborough, Easton, St. Michael's, and Baltimore. The people looked more able, stronger, healthier, and happier, than those of Maryland. I was for once made glad by a view of extreme wealth, without being saddened by seeing extreme poverty. But the most astonishing as well as the most interesting thing to me was the condition of the colored people, a great many of whom, like myself, had escaped thither as a refuge from the hunters of men. I found many, who had not been seven years out of their chains, living in finer houses, and evidently enjoying more of the comforts of life, than the average of slaveholders in Maryland. I will venture to assert that my friend Mr. Nathan Johnson (of whom I can say with a grateful heart, "I was hungry, and he gave me meat; I was thirsty, and he gave me drink; I was a stranger, and he took me in") lived in a neater house; dined at a better table; took, paid for, and read, more newspapers; better understood the moral, religious, and political character of the nation,—than nine tenths of the slave-holders in Talbot county, Maryland. Yet Mr. Johnson was a working man. His hands were hardened by toil, and not his alone, but those also of Mrs. Johnson. I found the colored people much more spirited than I had supposed they would be. I found among them a determination to protect each other from the blood-thirsty kidnapper, at all hazards. Soon after my arrival, I was told of a circumstance which illustrated their spirit. A colored man and a fugitive slave were on unfriendly terms. The former was heard to threaten the latter with informing his master of his whereabouts. Straightway a meeting was called among the colored people, under the stereotyped notice, "Business of importance!" The betrayer was invited to attend. The people came at the appointed hour, and organized the meeting by appointing a very religious old gentleman as president, who, I believe, made a prayer, after which he addressed the meeting as follows: *"Friends, we have got him here, and I would recommend that you young men just take him outside the door, and kill him!"* With this, a number of them bolted at him; but they were intercepted by some more timid than themselves, and the betrayer escaped their vengeance, and has not been seen in New Bedford since. I believe there have been no more such threats, and should there be hereafter, I doubt not that death would be the consequence.

I found employment, the third day after my arrival, in stowing a sloop with a load of oil. It was new, dirty, and hard work for me; but I went at it with a glad heart and a willing hand. I was now my own master. It was a happy moment, the rapture of which can be understood only by those who have been slaves. It was the first work, the reward of which was to be entirely my own. There was no Master Hugh standing ready, the moment I earned the money, to rob me of it. I worked that day with a pleasure I had never before experienced. I was at work for myself and newly-married wife. It was to me the starting-point of a new existence. When I got through with that job, I went in pursuit of a job of calking; but such was the strength of prejudice against color, among the white calkers, that they refused to work with me, and of course I could get no employment.[3] Finding my trade of no immediate benefit, I threw off my calking habiliments, and prepared myself to do any kind of work I could get to do. Mr. Johnson kindly let me have his wood-horse and saw, and I very soon found myself a plenty of work. There was no work too hard—none too dirty. I was ready to saw wood, shovel

---

3 I am told that colored persons can now get employment at calking in New Bedford—a result of anti-slavery effort.

coal, carry the hod, sweep the chimney, or roll oil casks,—all of which I did for nearly three years in New Bedford, before I became known to the anti-slavery world.

In about four months after I went to New Bedford, there came a young man to me, and inquired if I did not wish to take the "Liberator." I told him I did; but, just having made my escape from slavery, I remarked that I was unable to pay for it then. I, however, finally became a subscriber to it. The paper came, and I read it from week to week with such feelings as it would be quite idle for me to attempt to describe. The paper became my meat and my drink. My soul was set all on fire. Its sympathy for my brethren in bonds—its scathing denunciations of slaveholders—its faithful exposures of slavery—and its powerful attacks upon the upholders of the institution—sent a thrill of joy through my soul, such as I had never felt before!

I had not long been a reader of the "Liberator," before I got a pretty correct idea of the principles, measures and spirit of the anti-slavery reform. I took right hold of the cause. I could do but little; but what I could, I did with a joyful heart, and never felt happier than when in an anti-slavery meeting. I seldom had much to say at the meetings, because what I wanted to say was said so much better by others. But, while attending an anti-slavery convention at Nantucket, on the 11th of August, 1841, I felt strongly moved to speak, and was at the same time much urged to do so by Mr. William C. Coffin, a gentleman who had heard me speak in the colored people's meeting at New Bedford. It was a severe cross, and I took it up reluctantly. The truth was, I felt myself a slave, and the idea of speaking to white people weighed me down. I spoke but a few moments, when I felt a degree of freedom, and said what I desired with considerable ease. From that time until now, I have been engaged in pleading the cause of my brethren—with what success, and with what devotion, I leave those acquainted with my labors to decide.

APPENDIX

I FIND, SINCE reading over the foregoing Narrative, that I have, in several instances, spoken in such a tone and manner, respecting religion, as may possibly lead those unacquainted with my religious views to suppose me an opponent of all religion. To remove the liability of such misapprehension, I deem it proper to append the following brief explanation. What I have said respecting and against religion, I mean strictly to apply to the *slaveholding religion* of this land, and with no possible reference to Christianity proper; for, between the Christianity of this land, and the Christianity of Christ, I recognize the widest possible difference—so wide, that to receive the one as good, pure, and holy, is of necessity to reject the other as bad, corrupt, and wicked. To be the friend of the one, is of necessity to be the enemy of the other. I love the pure, peaceable, and impartial Christianity of Christ: I therefore hate the corrupt, slaveholding, women-whipping, cradle-plundering, partial and hypocritical Christianity of this land. Indeed, I can see no reason, but the most deceitful one, for calling the religion of this land Christianity. I look upon it as the climax of all misnomers, the boldest of all frauds, and the grossest of all libels. Never was there a clearer case of "stealing the livery of the court of heaven to serve the devil in." I am filled with unutterable loathing when I contemplate the religious pomp and show, together with the horrible inconsistencies, which every where surround me. We have men-stealers for ministers, women-whippers for missionaries, and cradle-plunderers for church members. The man who wields the blood-clotted cowskin during the week fills the pulpit on Sunday, and claims to be a minister of the meek and lowly Jesus. The man who robs me of my earnings at the end of each week meets me as a class-leader on Sunday morning, to show me the way of life, and the path of salvation. He who sells my sister, for purposes of prostitution, stands forth as the pious advocate of purity. He who proclaims it a religious duty to read the Bible denies me the right of learning to read the name of the God who made me. He who is the religious advocate of marriage robs whole millions of its sacred influence, and leaves them to the ravages of wholesale pollution. The warm defender of the sacredness of the family relation is the same that scatters whole families,—sundering husbands and wives, parents and children, sisters and brothers,—leaving the hut vacant, and the hearth desolate. We see the thief preaching against theft, and the adulterer against adultery. We have men sold to build churches, women sold to support the gospel, and babes sold to purchase Bibles for the *poor heathen! all for the glory of God and the good of souls!* The slave auctioneer's bell and the churchgoing bell chime in with each other, and the bitter cries of the heart-broken slave are drowned in the religious shouts of his pious master. Revivals of religion and revivals in the slave-trade go hand in hand together. The slave prison and the church stand near each other. The clanking of fetters and the rattling of chains in the prison, and the pious psalm and solemn prayer in the church, may be heard at the same time. The dealers in the bodies and souls of men erect their stand in the presence of the pulpit, and they mutually help each other. The dealer gives his blood-stained gold to support the pulpit, and the pulpit, in return, covers his infernal business with the garb of Christianity. Here we have religion and robbery the allies of each other— devils dressed in angels' robes, and hell presenting the semblance of paradise.

> "Just God! and these are they,
>   Who minister at thine altar, God of right!

Men who their hands, with prayer and blessing, lay
   On Israel's ark of light.

"What! preach, and kidnap men?
   Give thanks, and rob thy own afflicted poor?
Talk of thy glorious liberty, and then
   Bolt hard the captive's door?

"What! servants of thy own
   Merciful Son, who came to seek and save
The homeless and the outcast, fettering down
   The tasked and plundered slave!

"Pilate and Herod friends!
   Chief priests and rulers, as of old, combine!
Just God and holy! is that church which lends
   Strength to the spoiler thine?"

The Christianity of America is a Christianity, of whose votaries
it may be as truly said, as it was of the ancient scribes and
Pharisees, "They bind heavy burdens, and grievous to be borne,
and lay them on men's shoulders, but they themselves will not
move them with one of their fingers. All their works they do
for to be seen of men.—They love the uppermost rooms at feasts,
and the chief seats in the synagogues, . . . and to be called of
men, Rabbi, Rabbi.—But woe unto you, scribes and Pharisees,
hypocrites! for ye shut up the kingdom of heaven against men;
for ye neither go in yourselves, neither suffer ye them that are
entering to go in. Ye devour widows' houses, and for a pretence
make long prayers; therefore ye shall receive the greater dam-
nation. Ye compass sea and land to make one proselyte, and
when he is made, ye make him twofold more the child of hell
than yourselves.—Woe unto you, scribes and Pharisees, hypocrites! for ye pay tithe of mint, and anise, and cumin, and have
omitted the weightier matters of the law, judgment, mercy,

and faith; these ought ye to have done, and not to leave the other undone. Ye blind guides! which strain at a gnat, and swallow a camel.—Woe unto you, scribes and Pharisees, hypocrites! for ye make clean the outside of the cup and of the platter; but within, they are full of extortion and excess. Woe unto you, scribes and Pharisees, hypocrites! for ye are like unto whited sepulchres, which indeed appear beautiful outward, but are within full of dead men's bones, and of all uncleanness. Even so ye also outwardly appear righteous unto men, but within ye are full of hypocrisy and iniquity."

Dark and terrible as is this picture, I hold it to be strictly true of the overwhelming mass of professed Christians in America. They strain at a gnat, and swallow a camel. Could any thing be more true of our churches? They would be shocked at the proposition of fellowshipping a *sheep*-stealer, and at the same time they hug to their communion a *man*-stealer, and brand me with being an infidel, if I find fault with them for it. They attend with Pharisaical strictness to the outward forms of religion, and at the same time neglect the weightier matters of the law, judgment, mercy, and faith. They are always ready to sacrifice, but seldom to show mercy. They are they who are represented as professing to love God whom they have not seen, whilst they hate their brother whom they have seen. They love the heathen on the other side of the globe. They can pray for him, pay money to have the Bible put into his hand, and missionaries to instruct him; while they despise and totally neglect the heathen at their own doors.

Such is, very briefly, my view of the religion of this land; and to avoid any misunderstanding, growing out of the use of general terms, I mean, by the religion of this land, that which is revealed in the words, deeds, and actions, of those bodies, north and south, calling themselves Christian churches, and yet in union with slaveholders. It is against religion, as presented by these bodies, that I have felt it my duty to testify.

I conclude these remarks by copying the following portrait of the religion of the south, (which is, by communion and fellowship, the religion of the north,) which I soberly affirm is "true to the life," and without caricature or the slightest exaggeration. It is said to have been drawn, several years before the present anti-slavery agitation began, by a northern Methodist preacher, who, while residing at the south, had an opportunity to see slaveholding morals, manners, and piety, with his own eyes. "Shall I not visit for these things? saith the Lord. Shall not my soul be avenged on such a nation as this?"

"A PARODY

"Come, saints and sinners, hear me tell
How pious priests whip Jack and Nell,
And women buy and children sell,
And preach all sinners down to hell,
    And sing of heavenly union.

"They'll bleat and baa, dona like goats,
Gorge down black sheep, and strain at motes,
Array their backs in fine black coats,
Then seize their negroes by their throats,
    And choke, for heavenly union.

"They'll church you if you sip a dram,
And damn you if you steal a lamb;
Yet rob old Tony, Doll, and Sam,
Of human rights, and bread and ham;
    Kidnapper's heavenly union.

"They'll loudly talk of Christ's reward,
And bind his image with a cord,

And scold, and swing the lash abhorred,
And sell their brother in the Lord
   To handcuffed heavenly union.

"They'll read and sing a sacred song,
And make a prayer both loud and long,
And teach the right and do the wrong,
Hailing the brother, sister throng,
   With words of heavenly union.

"We wonder how such saints can sing,
Or praise the Lord upon the wing,
Who roar, and scold, and whip, and sting,
And to their slaves and mammon cling,
   In guilty conscience union.

"They'll raise tobacco, corn, and rye,
And drive, and thieve, and cheat, and lie,
And lay up treasures in the sky,
By making switch and cowskin fly,
   In hope of heavenly union.

"They'll crack old Tony on the skull,
And preach and roar like Bashan bull,
Or braying ass, of mischief full,
Then seize old Jacob by the wool,
   And pull for heavenly union.

"A roaring, ranting, sleek man-thief,
Who lived on mutton, veal, and beef,
Yet never would afford relief
To needy, sable sons of grief,
   Was big with heavenly union.

" 'Love not the world,' the preacher said,
And winked his eye, and shook his head;
He seized on Tom, and Dick, and Ned,
Cut short their meat, and clothes, and bread,
    Yet still loved heavenly union.

"Another preacher whining spoke
Of One whose heart for sinners broke:
He tied old Nanny to an oak,
And drew the blood at every stroke,
    And prayed for heavenly union.

"Two others oped their iron jaws,
And waved their children-stealing paws;
There sat their children in gewgaws;
By stinting negroes' backs and maws,
    They kept up heavenly union.

"All good from Jack another takes,
And entertains their flirts and rakes,
Who dress as sleek as glossy snakes,
And cram their mouths with sweetened cakes;
    And this goes down for union."

Sincerely and earnestly hoping that this little book may do
something toward throwing light on the American slave system,
and hastening the glad day of deliverance to the millions of my
brethren in bonds—faithfully relying upon the power of truth,
love, and justice, for success in my humble efforts—and solemnly
pledging myself anew to the sacred cause,—I subscribe myself,

FREDERICK DOUGLASS

Lynn, *Mass., April* 28, 1845

Speeches

WE HAVE DECIDED TO STAY
(1848)

In this speech, Frederick Douglass addresses the policy of "Colonization" supported by many anti-slavery Americans (including, and especially, Abraham Lincoln) in which freed slaves would be voluntarily returned to Africa. It was delivered before the American Anti-Slavery Society in New York City on May 9, 1848.

MR. CHAIRMAN, AND Ladies, and Gentlemen:

It is with great hesitation that I consent to rise here to speak, after the able speech to which you have just listened. I had far rather remain a listener to others, than to become myself a speaker at this stage of the proceedings of this meeting. I do not hope to be able, in the few remarks I have to make, to say anything new or eloquent, for it will be time indeed to discuss new truths, when old ones shall have been recognized and adopted.

For seventeen years, Mr. Chairman, the Abolitionists of the United States have been encountering obloquy, scorn, and opposition of the most furious character, for uttering,—what? Their conviction that a man is a man,—that every man belongs to himself and to no one else. In propagating this idea, this simple proposition, we have met with all sorts of opposition, and with all sorts of arguments drawn from the Bible, from the Constitution, and from philosophy, till at length many have arrived at the sage conclusion that a man is something else than a man, and that he has not the rights of a man.

An event has just occurred in the District of Columbia, the Capitol of the country, known to you all, which furnishes the proof of this assertion. Some seventy-seven men, women, and children, took it into their heads, contrary to the Constitution, that they were men, not three-fifths of men—that they would leave the refined avocation of blacking boots for nothing for members of Congress, and seek an asylum from oppression and tyranny in some of the Northern States, or under the protection of the British Lion in Canada. The sequel is well known; they were pursued by a band of armed men, overtaken, and brought back in chains, and the men who aided them in their flight are in a dungeon, and there they will probably end their lives.

Very little is thought about this affair,—very little noise is made about it. It excites about as much remark, and about as much sympathy as if as many horses had broken away from the halters of their owners, and again been recovered.

Sir, we have, in this country, no adequate idea of humanity yet; the nation does not feel that these are men, it cannot see through the dark skin and curly hair of the black man, anything like humanity, or that has claims to human rights. Had they been white men and women, or were they regarded as human beings, this nation would have been agitated to its centre, and rocked as with an earthquake shock, and like the nations of the Old World, would have rung with the thunders of freedom against tyranny, at such an event as this.

We do not regard these men as formed in the image of God. We do not see that in the persons of these men and women whose rights have been stricken down, whose virtuous attempt to gain their freedom, has been defeated, the violation of the common rights of man.

Even the gallant Hale, of the Liberty party, does not dare to speak of the men who aided their escape, as having done a noble deed. To be sure, he can bring in a proposition for the better protection of property in the District of Columbia, but he makes no allusion whatever, to the rights of black men. This proposition in relation to the rights of property, is regarded by his adherents as a noble act; as a timely measure; as indicating great courage and heroism. Nor do I care to deny it. But what is the inference? If it be a noble act, a courageous act, to move in the Capitol of the nation, in the Senate of the United States, a bill to protect property from the assaults of a brutal and ferocious mob,—if that be bold, of course it would be no less daring and fanatical to move in that District, that the rights of man be protected.

I do not propose to make a lengthy speech, but I would like to say a few words about how these things look to others.

> "O wad some power the giftie gie us
> To see oursels as others see us."

I would like to hold up to you a picture; not drawn by an American pen or pencil, but by a foreigner. I want to show you how you look abroad in the delectable business of kidnapping and slave driving.

Sometimes since—I think it was in the December number of "Punch,"—I saw an excellent pictorial description of America.—What think you it was? It was entitled, "Brother Jonathan." It was a long, lean, gaunt, shriveled looking creature, stretched out on two chairs, and his legs resting on the prostrate bust of Washington; projecting from behind was a cat-o'-nine tails knotted at the ends; around his person he wore a belt in which were stuck those truly American implements, a bowie knife, dirk, and revolving pistol; behind him was a whipping post, with a naked woman tied to it, and a strong-armed American citizen in the act of scourging her livid flesh with a cowskin. At his feet was another group;—a sale going on, of human cattle, and around the auctioneer's table were gathered the respectability,—the religion represented in the person of the clergy,—of America, buying them for export to the goodly city of New Orleans. Little further on there was a scene of branding,—a small group of slaves tied hand and foot, while their patriotic and philanthropic masters were burning their name into their quivering flesh. Further on, there was a drove of slaves, bound for New Orleans. Above these and several other scenes illustrative of the character of our institutions, waved the star spangled banner. Still further back in the distance was the picture of the achievements of our gallant army in Mexico, shooting, stabbing, hanging; destroying property, and massacring the innocent with the innocent, not with the guilty, and over all this was a picture of the Devil himself, looking down with Satanic satisfaction on passing events.

Here I conceive to be a true picture of America, and I hesitate not to say that this description falls far short of the real facts, and of the aspect we bear to the world around us.

Sir, although we have heard conflicting views uttered here today, of hopeful and desponding aspects, (if, indeed, we have any desponding aspects brought to us,) still, I think much more may be said in behalf of the hopeful aspects. The signs of the times have been already alluded to; we have very properly gone beyond the limits of the United States.

I see some of the audience are going out, which makes me think I have spoken long enough; some plants thrive better by being cut off, and perhaps my speech may as well be cut off here; not because there is not more to be said, but because your energies have been taxed quite enough already. Since, then, you wish me to proceed, and, as Henry Clay says, "I am always subject to the will of the people," there may yet be room for something of a speech.

As I was proceeding to remark concerning the hopeful aspects of the times, I wish to bring with more distinctness before your minds, the news which comes from abroad—the action of the Provisional Government of France. We have been accustomed, in this country, to hear much talk about "Christian America, and Infidel France." I want to say in behalf of France, that I go for that infidelity—no matter how heinous it may be in the estimation of the American people—which strikes the chains from the limbs of our brethren; and against that Christianity which puts them on,—for that infidelity, which, in the person of Cremieux, one of the members of the Provisional Government of France, speaks to the black and mulatto men, that come to congratulate them, and express their sentiments upon the immediate emancipation of their brethren in the French islands. I sympathize with that infidelity that speaks to them in language like this: friends! brothers! men! In France, the Negro is a man, while you who are throwing up your caps, and waving your banners, and making beautiful speeches in behalf of liberty, deny us our humanity, and traffic in our flesh.

Sir, I would like to bring more vividly to before this audience, the wrongs of my downtrodden countrymen. I have no disposition to look at this matter in any sentimental light, but to bring before you stern facts, and keep forever before the American people the damning and disgraceful fact, that three millions of people are in chains today—that while we are here speaking in their behalf, saying noble words and doing noble deeds, they are under the yoke, smarting beneath the lash, sundered from each other, trafficked in and brutally treated; and that the American nation, to keep them in their present condition, stands ready with its ten thousand bayonets, to plunge them into their hearts. If they attempt to strike for their freedom, I want every man north of Mason and Dixon's line, whenever they attend an anti-slavery meeting, to remember that it is the Northern area that does this—that you are not only guilty of withholding your influence, but that you are the positive enemies of the slave, the positive holders of the slave, and that in your right arm rests the physical power that keeps him under the yoke.

I want you to feel that I am addressing slaveholders; speaking to men who have entered into a solemn league and covenant with the slaveholders of the country, that in any emergency, if at any time the spirit of freedom finds a lodgment in the bosom of the American slave, and they shall be moved to throw up barricades against their tyrants, as the French did in the streets of Paris, that you, every man of you that swears to support the Constitution, is sworn to pour leaden death into their hearts. I am speaking to slaveholders, and if I speak plainly, set it not down to impudence, but to opposition to Slavery. For God's sake, let a man speak when he cannot do anything else; when fetters are on his limbs, let him have this small right of making his wrongs known; at least, let it be done in New York. I am glad to see there is a disposition to let it be done here—to allow him to tell what is in him, with regard to his own personal wrongs at any rate.

Sir, I have been frequently denounced because I have dared to speak against the American nation, against the Church—the Northern churches especially, charging them with being the slaveholders of the country. I desire to say here, as elsewhere, that I am not at all ambitious of the ill opinions of my countrymen, nor do I desire their hatred; but I must say, as I have said, that I want no man's friendship, no matter how high he may stand in Church or State, I want no man's sympathies or approbation who is not ready to strike the chains from the limbs of my brethren. I do not ask the esteem and friendship of any minister or any man, no matter how high his standing, nor do I wish to shake any man's hand, who stands indifferent to the wrongs of my brethren. Some have boasted that when Fred Douglass has been at their houses, he has been treated kindly, but as soon as he got into their pulpits he began to abuse them— that as soon as the advantage is given him, he takes it to stab those who befriend him. Friends, I wish to stab no man, but if you stand on the side of the slaveholder, and cry out "the Union as it is," "the Constitution as it is," "the Church as it is," you may expect that the heart that throbs beneath this bosom, will give utterance against you. I am bound to speak, and, whenever there is an opportunity to do so, I will speak against Slavery.

I meant to have said a word about Colonization, as I observed there was a very dark-looking individual here, (Gov. Pinney, of Liberia,) for whose special benefit I wished to say something on that subject. But as I do not see him here now, there is no necessity to discuss this subject for his benefit. When he was pointed out to me, I thought it remarkable, that so dark a man should be in favor of colonization; but there are some simple-minded men even among colored people. I will just say, however, that we have had some advice given us lately, from very high authority. I allude to Henry Clay, who in his last speech before the Colonization Society, at Washington, advised the free colored people of the United States that they had better go to Africa.

He says he does not wish to coerce us, but thinks we had better go! What right has he to tell us to go? We have as much right to stay here as he has. I don't care if you did throw up your caps for him when he came to this city—I don't care if he did give you "his heart on the outside of the city Hall and his hand on the inside;" I have as much right to stay here as he has! And I want to say to our white friends, that we, colored folks, have had the subject under consideration, and have decided to stay! want to say to any colonization friends here, that they may give their minds no further uneasiness on our account, for our minds are made up. I think this is about the best argument on that subject.

Now there is one thing more about us colored folks; it is this, that under all these most adverse circumstances, we live and move and have our being, and that too in peace, and are almost persuaded that there is a providence in our staying here. I do not know but the United States would rot in its tyranny, if there were not some Negroes in this land—some to clink their chains in the care of listening humanity, and from whose prostrate forms the lessons of liberty can be taught to the whites.

It is through us now that you are learning that your own rights are stricken down.—At this time it is the Abolitionist that holds up the lamp that shows the political parties of the North their fetters and chains. A little while ago, and the

Northern men were bound in the strange fanatic delusion, that they had something to do with making of Presidents of the United States: that is about given up now. No one now of common sense, or common reading, imagines for a moment that New York has anything to do with deciding who the President shall be. They are allowed to vote, but what is the amount of this privilege? It is to vote for the slaveholder, or whom the slaveholders select.

No men that are now accounted sane, think of any other than of a slaveholder or assassin, or both, who shall hold the destinies of the nation,—and the reason is because the people are convinced that they belong—as they used to say to the colored boys of the South, to the party. They used sometimes to ask me, "boy who do you belong to?" and I used to answer "to Captain Thomas Auld, of St. Michael's, a class-leader in the Methodist Episcopal church;" and now I would ask, "who do you belong to?" I will tell you. You belong to the Democratic party, to the Whig party, and these parties belong to the slaveholder, and the slaveholder rules the country. As the boy said about ruling England: "I rule mamma, and mamma rules papa, and papa rules the people, and the people rule England." To be sure you have the right to vote, which is like what I heard once of a certain boy, who said he was going to live with his uncle Robert, and when I go there, said he, I am going to do just as I please—if uncle Robert will let me!

The Northern people are going to do just as they please if the slaveholders will let them. The little bit of opposition that has manifested itself in that little protuberance on American politics—the Wilmot proviso—which our friend Gay has fully described as a tempest in a teapot, has now quite flattened down. The Whigs, who said we will stand by it at all hazards, have fairly backed out; they did so last fall; they got afraid of the Union. In Ohio I heard men striking their fists together, saying they would stand by it at all hazards; and after a little while, the Ohio State Legislature come to the conclusion, after having carefully considered the matter, that "to press the question of no more slave territory must be disastrous to our American Union."—New York came out expressly in favor of the Proviso and it has since seen that the Union will be periled by adherence to that principle. And all over the North there is this fainting away before that power which was before undefined, as has been so eloquently touched upon by my friend Phillips; for while men hold up their hands in favor of the Union and the Constitution, there is a moral conflict in their hearts, for, as was so beautifully expressed by Mr. Parker, of Boston, men cannot fight Slavery under the Constitution; the Constitution soils the amour about them; we cannot strike Slavery while we have it on us: there is no other way to throw it off.

I have no prepared speech, and I will not weary you any longer. I have sometimes thought since the late occurrences in France, that there may be an under current in men's hearts here as there was in Paris; Louis Philippe thought himself perfectly secure surrounded by his 300,000 soldiers, who, with fixed bayonets, were ready to support him in the suppression of the riots; but the troops were found to fraternize with the people; the soldier joined the civilian to assert and defend his rights. So I believe here, after all we have said against the American people, there is yet an under current pervading the mass of the people in this country, uniting Democrat and Whig, and men of no party, taking hold in quarters we know not of, which shall one day rise up in one glorious Fraternity for Freedom, uniting into one mighty phalanx of freemen to bring down the haughty citadel of Slavery with all its bloody towers and turrets.

> "There's a good time coming boys,
> A good time coming,
> Wait a little longer.
> We may not live to see the day,

But earth shall glisten in the ray
Of the good time coming;
Cannon balls may aid the truth,
But thought's a weapon stronger,
We'll win our battle by its aid,
Wait a little longer."

What the Black Man Wants
(1865)

In one of his most famous speeches, Frederick Douglas lays out his argument on why African Americans both desire and deserve not mere "generosity," but full equality and suffrage under the law. Delivered within days of Lincoln's assassination and the end of the civil war, this speech took place in early April of 1865 at the Annual Meeting of the Massachusetts Anti-Slavery Society in Boston.

I CAME HERE, as I come always to the meetings in New England, as a listener, and not as a speaker; and one of the reasons why I have not been more frequently to the meetings of this society, has been because of the disposition on the part of some of my friends to call me out upon the platform, even when they knew that there was some difference of opinion and of feeling between those who rightfully belong to this platform and myself; and for fear of being misconstrued, as desiring to interrupt or disturb the proceedings of these meetings, I have usually kept away, and have thus been deprived of that educating influence, which I am always free to confess is of the highest order, descending from this platform. I have felt, since I have lived out West[1], that in going there I parted from a great deal that was valuable; and I feel, every time I come to these meetings, that I have lost a great deal by making my home west of Boston, west of Massachusetts; for, if anywhere in the country there is to be found the highest sense of justice, or the truest demands for my

---

1 Douglass means west of Boston, in Rochester, NY.

race, I look for it in the East, I look for it here. The ablest discussions of the whole question of our rights occur here, and to be deprived of the privilege of listening to those discussions is a great deprivation.

I do not know, from what has been said, that there is any difference of opinion as to the duty of abolitionists, at the present moment. How can we get up any difference at this point, or any point, where we are so united, so agreed? I went especially, however, with that word of Mr. Phillips, which is the criticism of Gen. Banks and Gen. Banks' policy.[2] I hold that that policy is our chief danger at the present moment; that it practically enslaves the Negro, and makes the Proclamation[3] of 1863 a mockery and delusion. What is freedom? It is the right to choose one's own employment. Certainly it means that, if it means anything; and when any individual or combination of individuals undertakes to decide for any man when he shall work, where he shall work, at what he shall work, and for what he shall work, he or they practically reduce him to slavery. He is a slave. That I understand Gen. Banks to do—to determine for the so-called freedman, when, and where, and at what, and for how much he shall work, when he shall be punished, and by whom punished. It is absolute slavery. It defeats the beneficent intention of the Government, if it has beneficent intentions, in regards to the freedom of our people.

I have had but one idea for the last three years to present to the American people, and the phraseology in which I clothe it is the old abolition phraseology. I am for the "immediate, unconditional, and universal" enfranchisement of the black man, in every State in the Union. Without this, his liberty is a mockery;

---

2 Gen. Banks instituted a labor policy in Louisiana that was discriminatory of blacks, claiming that it was to help prepare them to better handle freedom. Wendell Phillips countered by saying, "If there is anything patent in the whole history of our thirty years' struggle, it is that the Negro no more needs to be prepared for liberty than the white man."
3 The Emancipation Proclamation.

without this, you might as well almost retain the old name of slavery for his condition; for in fact, if he is not the slave of the individual master, he is the slave of society, and holds his liberty as a privilege, not as a right. He is at the mercy of the mob, and has no means of protecting himself.

It may be objected, however, that this pressing of the Negro's right to suffrage is premature. Let us have slavery abolished, it may be said, let us have labor organized, and then, in the natural course of events, the right of suffrage will be extended to the Negro. I do not agree with this. The constitution of the human mind is such, that if it once disregards the conviction forced upon it by a revelation of truth, it requires the exercise of a higher power to produce the same conviction afterwards. The American people are now in tears. The Shenandoah has run blood—the best blood of the North. All around Richmond, the blood of New England and of the North has been shed—of your sons, your brothers and your fathers. We all feel, in the existence of this Rebellion, that judgments terrible, wide-spread, far-reaching, overwhelming, are abroad in the land; and we feel, in view of these judgments, just now, a disposition to learn righteousness. This is the hour. Our streets are in mourning, tears are falling at every fireside, and under the chastisement of this Rebellion we have almost come up to the point of conceding this great, this all-important right of suffrage. I fear that if we fail to do it now, if abolitionists fail to press it now, we may not see, for centuries to come, the same disposition that exists at this moment. Hence, I say, now is the time to press this right.

It may be asked, "Why do you want it? Some men have got along very well without it. Women have not this right." Shall we justify one wrong by another? This is the sufficient answer. Shall we at this moment justify the deprivation of the Negro of the right to vote, because some one else is deprived of that privilege? I hold that women, as well as men, have the right to vote, and my heart and voice go with the movement to extend suffrage to woman; but that question rests upon another basis than which our right rests. We may be asked, I say, why we want it. I will tell you why we want it. We want it because it is our right, first of all. No class of men can, without insulting their own nature, be content with any deprivation of their rights. We want it again, as a means for educating our race. Men are so constituted that they derive their conviction of their own possibilities largely by the estimate formed of them by others. If nothing is expected of a people, that people will find it difficult to contradict that expectation. By depriving us of suffrage, you affirm our incapacity to form an intelligent judgment respecting public men and public measures; you declare before the world that we are unfit to exercise the elective franchise, and by this means lead us to undervalue ourselves, to put a low estimate upon ourselves, and to feel that we have no possibilities like other men. Again, I want the elective franchise, for one, as a colored man, because ours is a peculiar government, based upon a peculiar idea, and that idea is universal suffrage. If I were in a monarchial government, or an autocratic or aristocratic government, where the few bore rule and the many were subject, there would be no special stigma resting upon me, because I did not exercise the elective franchise. It would do me no great violence. Mingling with the mass I should partake of the strength of the mass; I should be supported by the mass, and I should have the same incentives to endeavor with the mass of my fellow-men; it would be no particular burden, no particular deprivation; but here where universal suffrage is the rule, where that is the fundamental idea of the Government, to rule us out is to make us an exception, to brand us with the stigma of inferiority, and to invite to our heads the missiles of those about us; therefore, I want the franchise for the black man.

There are, however, other reasons, not derived from any consideration merely of our rights, but arising out of the conditions of the South, and of the country—considerations which have already been referred to by Mr. Phillips—considerations which must arrest the attention of statesmen. I believe that when the tall heads of this Rebellion shall have been swept down, as they will be swept down, when the Davises and Toombses and Stephenses, and others who are leading this Rebellion shall have been blotted out, there will be this rank undergrowth of treason, to which reference has been made, growing up there, and interfering with, and thwarting the quiet operation of the Federal Government in those states. You will see those traitors, handing down, from sire to son, the same malignant spirit which they have manifested and which they are now exhibiting, with malicious hearts, broad blades, and bloody hands in the field, against our sons and brothers. That spirit will still remain; and whoever sees the Federal Government extended over those Southern States will see that Government in a strange land, and not only in a strange land, but in an enemy's land. A postmaster of the United States in the South will find himself surrounded by a hostile spirit; a collector in a Southern port will find himself surrounded by a hostile spirit; a United States marshal or United States judge will be surrounded there by a hostile element. That enmity will not die out in a year, will not die out in an age. The Federal Government will be looked upon in those States precisely as the Governments of Austria and France are looked upon in Italy at the present moment. They will endeavor to circumvent, they will endeavor to destroy, the peaceful operation of this Government. Now, where will you find the strength to counterbalance this spirit, if you do not find it in the Negroes of the South? They are your friends, and have always been your friends. They were your friends even when the Government did not regard them as such. They comprehended the genius of this war before you did. It is a significant fact, it is a marvelous fact, it seems almost to imply a direct interposition of Providence, that this war, which began in the interest of slavery on both sides, bids fair to end in the interest of liberty on both sides. It was begun, I say, in the interest of slavery on both sides. The South was fighting to take slavery out of the Union, and the North was fighting to keep it in the Union; the South fighting to get it beyond the limits of the United States Constitution, and the North fighting to retain it within those limits; the South fighting for new guarantees, and the North fighting for the old guarantees;—both despising the Negro, both insulting the Negro. Yet, the Negro, apparently endowed with wisdom from on high, saw more clearly the end from the beginning than we did. When Seward said the status of no man in the country would be changed by the war, the Negro did not believe him. When our generals sent their underlings in shoulder-straps to hunt the flying Negro back from our lines into the jaws of slavery, from which he had escaped, the Negroes thought that a mistake had been made, and that the intentions of the Government had not been rightly understood by our officers in shoulder-straps, and they continued to come into our lines, threading their way through bogs and fens, over briers and thorns, fording streams, swimming rivers, bringing us tidings as to the safe path to march, and pointing out the dangers that threatened us. They are our only friends in the South, and we should be true to them in this, their trial hour, and see to it that they have the elective franchise.

I know that we are inferior to you in some things—virtually inferior. We walk about you like dwarfs among giants. Our heads are scarcely seen above the great sea of humanity. The Germans are superior to us; the Irish are superior to us; the Yankees are superior to us; they can do what we cannot, that is, what we have not hitherto been allowed to do. But while I make this admission, I utterly deny, that we are originally, or naturally, or practically, or in any way, or in any important sense, inferior to anybody on this globe. This charge of inferiority is an old dodge. It has been made available for oppression on many occasions. It is only about six centuries since the blue-eyed and fair-haired Anglo-Saxons were considered inferior by the haughty Normans, who once trampled upon them. If you read the history of the Norman Conquest, you will find that this proud Anglo-Saxon was once looked upon as of coarser clay than his Norman master, and might be found in the highways and byways of Old England laboring with a brass collar on his neck, and the name of his master marked upon it. You were down then! You are up now. I am glad you are up, and I want you to be glad to help us up also.

The story of our inferiority is an old dodge, as I have said; for wherever men oppress their fellows, wherever they enslave them, they will endeavor to find the needed apology for such enslavement and oppression in the character of the people oppressed and enslaved. When we wanted, a few years ago, a slice of Mexico, it was hinted that the Mexicans were an inferior race, that the old Castilian blood had become so weak that it would scarcely run down hill, and that Mexico needed the long, strong and beneficent arm of the Anglo-Saxon care extended over it. We said that it was necessary to its salvation, and a part of the "manifest destiny" of this Republic, to extend our arm over that dilapidated government. So, too, when Russia wanted to take possession of a part of the Ottoman Empire, the Turks were an "inferior race." So, too, when England wants to set the heel of her power more firmly in the quivering heart of old Ireland, the Celts are an "inferior race." So, too, the Negro, when he is to be robbed of any right which is justly his, is an "inferior man." It is said that we are ignorant; I admit it. But if we know enough to be hung, we know enough to vote. If the Negro knows enough to pay taxes to support the government, he knows enough to vote; taxation and representation should go together. If he knows enough to shoulder a musket and fight for the flag, fight for the government, he knows enough to vote. If he knows as much when he is sober as an Irishman knows when drunk, he knows enough to vote, on good American principles.

But I was saying that you needed a counterpoise in the persons of the slaves to the enmity that would exist at the South after the Rebellion is put down. I hold that the American people are bound, not only in self-defense, to extend this right to the freedmen of the South, but they are bound by their love of country, and by all their regard for the future safety of those Southern States, to do this—to do it as a measure essential to the preservation of peace there. But I will not dwell upon this. I put it to the American sense of honor. The honor of a nation is an important thing. It is said in the Scriptures, "What doth it profit a man if he gain the whole world, and lose his own soul?" It may be said, also, What doth it profit a nation if it gain the whole world, but lose its honor? I hold that the American government has taken upon itself a solemn obligation of honor, to see that this war—let it be long or short, let it cost much or let it cost little—that this war shall not cease until every freedman at the South has the right to vote. It has bound itself to it. What have you asked the black men of the South, the black men of the whole country to do? Why, you have asked them to incur the enmity of their masters, in order to befriend you and to befriend this Government. You have asked us to call down, not only upon ourselves, but upon our children's children, the deadly hate of the entire Southern people. You have called upon us to turn our backs upon our masters, to abandon their cause and espouse yours; to turn against the South and in favor of the North; to shoot down the Confederacy and uphold the flag— the American flag. You have called upon us to expose ourselves to all the subtle machinations of their malignity for all time. And now, what do you propose to do when you come to make peace? To reward your enemies, and trample in the dust your friends? Do you intend to sacrifice the very men who have come to the rescue of your banner in the South, and incurred the lasting displeasure of their masters thereby? Do you intend to sacrifice them and reward your enemies? Do you mean to give your enemies the right to vote, and take it away from your friends? Is that wise policy? Is that honorable? Could American honor withstand such a blow? I do not believe you will do it. I think you will see to it that we have the right to vote. There is something too mean in looking upon the Negro, when you are in trouble, as a citizen, and when you are free from trouble, as an alien. When this nation was in trouble, in its early struggles, it looked upon the Negro as a citizen. In 1776 he was a citizen. At the time of the formation of the

Constitution the Negro had the right to vote in eleven States out of the old thirteen. In your trouble you have made us citizens. In 1812 Gen. Jackson addressed us as citizens—"fellow-citizens." He wanted us to fight. We were citizens then! And now, when you come to frame a conscription bill, the Negro is a citizen again. He has been a citizen just three times in the history of this government, and it has always been in time of trouble. In time of trouble we are citizens. Shall we be citizens in war, and aliens in peace? Would that be just?

I ask my friends who are apologizing for not insisting upon this right, where can the black man look, in this country, for the assertion of his right, if he may not look to the Massachusetts Anti-Slavery Society? Where under the whole heavens can he look for sympathy, in asserting this right, if he may not look to this platform? Have you lifted us up to a certain height to see that we are men, and then are any disposed to leave us there, without seeing that we are put in possession of all our rights? We look naturally to this platform for the assertion of all our rights, and for this one especially. I understand the anti-slavery societies of this country to be based on two principles,—first, the freedom of the blacks of this country; and, second, the elevation of them. Let me not be misunderstood here. I am not asking for sympathy at the hands of abolitionists, sympathy at the hands of any. I think the American people are disposed often to be generous rather than just. I look over this country at the present time, and I see Educational Societies, Sanitary Commissions, Freedmen's Associations, and the like,—all very good: but in regard to the colored people there is always more that is benevolent, I perceive, than just, manifested towards us. What I ask for the Negro is not benevolence, not pity, not sympathy, but simply justice. The American people have always been anxious to know what they shall do with us. Gen. Banks was distressed with solicitude as to what he should do with the Negro. Everybody has asked the question, and they learned to ask it early of the abolitionists, "What shall we do with the

Negro?" I have had but one answer from the beginning. Do nothing with us! Your doing with us has already played the mischief with us. Do nothing with us! If the apples will not remain on the tree of their own strength, if they are worm-eaten at the core, if they are early ripe and disposed to fall, let them fall! I am not for tying or fastening them on the tree in any way, except by nature's plan, and if they will not stay there, let them fall. And if the Negro cannot stand on his own legs, let him fall also. All I ask is, give him a chance to stand on his own legs! Let him alone! If you see him on his way to school, let him alone, don't disturb him! If you see him going to the dinner table at a hotel, let him go! If you see him going to the ballot-box, let him alone, don't disturb him! If you see him going into a work-shop, just let him alone,—your interference is doing him a positive injury. Gen. Banks' "preparation" is of a piece with this attempt to prop up the Negro. Let him fall if he cannot stand alone! If the Negro cannot live by the line of eternal justice, so beautifully pictured to you in the illustration used by Mr. Phillips, the fault will not be yours, it will be his who made the Negro, and established that line for his government. [Applause.] Let him live or die by that. If you will only untie his hands, and give him a chance, I think he will live. He will work as readily for himself as the white man. A great many delusions have been swept away by this war. One was, that the Negro would not work; he has proved his ability to work. Another was, that the Negro would not fight; that he possessed only the most sheepish attributes of humanity; was a perfect lamb, or an "Uncle Tom;" disposed to take off his coat whenever required, fold his hands, and be whipped by anybody who wanted to whip him. But the war has proved that there is a great deal of human nature in the Negro, and that "he will fight," as Mr. Quincy, our President, said, in earlier days than these, "when there is reasonable probability of his whipping anybody."

JOHN BROWN
(1881)

John Brown gained notoriety throughout the 1850s as a revolutionary abolitionist who advocated armed rebellion as a means for ending the practice of slavery in the United States. He was executed shortly after leading 18 men on a raid of the Harpers Ferry Armory in 1859. In the following speech, delivered on May 30, 1881 at the Fourteenth Anniversary of Storer College, Douglass discusses the lasting impact of John Brown's life on the history of Slavery in America.

NOT TO FAN the flame of sectional animosity now happily in the process of rapid and I hope permanent extinction, not to revive and keep alive a sense of shame and remorse for a great national crime, which has brought its own punishment, in loss of treasure, tears and blood, not to recount the long list of wrongs, inflicted on my race during more than two hundred years of merciless bondage; nor yet to draw, from the labyrinths of far-off centuries, incidents and achievements wherewith to rouse your passions, and enkindle your enthusiasm, but to pay a just debt long due, to vindicate in some degree a great historical character, of our own time and country, one with whom I was myself well acquainted, and whose friendship and confidence it was my good fortune to share, and to give you such recollections, impressions and facts, as I can, of a grand, brave and good old man, and especially to promote a better understanding of the raid upon Harper's Ferry of which he was the chief, is the object of this address.

In all the thirty years' conflict with slavery, if we except the late tremendous war, there is no subject which in its interest and importance will be remembered longer, or will form a more thrilling chapter in American history than this strange, wild, bloody and mournful drama. The story of it is still fresh in the minds of many who now hear me, but for the sake of those who may have forgotten its details, and in order to have our subject in its entire range more fully and clearly before us at the outset, I will briefly state the facts in that extraordinary transaction.

On the night of the 16th of October, 1859, there appeared near the confluence of the Potomac and Shenandoah rivers, a party of nineteen men—fourteen white and five colored. They were not only armed themselves, but had brought with them a large supply of arms for such persons as might join them. These men invaded Harper's Ferry, disarmed the watchman, took possession of the arsenal, rifle-factory, armory and other government property at that place, arrested and made prisoners nearly all the prominent citizens of the neighborhood, collected about fifty slaves, put bayonets into the hands of such as were able and willing to fight for their liberty, killed three men, proclaimed general emancipation, held the ground more than thirty hours, were subsequently overpowered and nearly all killed, wounded or captured, by a body of United States troops, under command of Colonel Robert E. Lee, since famous as the rebel Gen. Lee. Three out of the nineteen invaders were captured whilst fighting, and one of these was Captain John Brown, the man who originated, planned and commanded the expedition. At the time of his capture Capt. Brown was supposed to be mortally wounded, as he had several ugly gashes and bayonet wounds on his head and body; and apprehending that he might speedily die, or that he might be rescued by his friends, and thus the opportunity of making him a signal example of slaveholding vengeance would be lost, his captors hurried him to Charlestown two miles further within the border of Virginia, placed him in prison strongly guarded by troops, and before his wounds were healed he was brought into court, subjected to a nominal trial, convicted of high treason and inciting slaves to insurrection, and was executed. His corpse was given to his woe-stricken widow, and she, assisted by Antislavery friends, caused it to be borne to North Elba, Essex County, NY, and there his dust now reposes, amid the silent, solemn and snowy grandeur of the Adirondacks.

Such is the story; with no line softened or hardened to my inclining. It certainly is not a story to please, but to pain. It is not a story to increase our sense of social safety and security, but to fill the imagination with wild and troubled fancies of doubt and danger. It was a sudden and startling surprise to the people of Harper's Ferry, and it is not easy to conceive of a situation more abundant in all the elements of horror and consternation. They had retired as usual to rest, with no suspicion that an enemy lurked in the surrounding darkness. They had quietly and trustingly given themselves up to "tired Nature's sweet restorer, balmy sleep," and while thus all unconscious of danger, they were roused from their peaceful slumbers by the sharp crack of the invader's rifle, and felt the keen-edged sword of war at their throats, three of their number being already slain.

Every feeling of the human heart was naturally outraged at this occurrence, and hence at the moment the air was full of denunciation and execration. So intense was this feeling, that few ventured to whisper a word of apology. But happily reason has her voice as well as feeling, and though slower in deciding, her judgments are broader, deeper, clearer and more enduring. It is not easy to reconcile human feeling to the shedding of blood for any purpose, unless indeed in the excitement which the shedding of blood itself occasions. The knife is to feeling always an offence. Even when in the hands of a skillful surgeon, it refuses consent to the operation long after reason has demonstrated its necessity. It even pleads the cause of the known murderer on the day of his execution, and calls society half criminal when, in cold blood, it takes life as a protection of itself from crime. Let no word be said against this holy feeling; more than to law and government are we indebted to this tender sentiment of regard for human life for the safety with which we walk the streets by day and sleep secure in our beds at night. It is nature's grand police, vigilant and faithful, sentineled in the soul, guarding against violence to peace and life. But whilst so much is freely accorded to feeling in the economy of human welfare, something more than feeling is necessary to grapple with a fact so grim and significant as was this raid. Viewed apart and alone, as a transaction separate and distinct from its antecedents and bearings, it takes rank with the most cold-blooded and atrocious wrongs ever perpetrated; but just here is the trouble—this raid on Harper's Ferry, no more than Sherman's march to the sea can consent to be thus viewed alone.

There is, in the world's government, a force which has in all ages been recognized, sometimes as Nemesis, sometimes as the judgment of God and sometimes as retributive justice; but under whatever name, all history attests the wisdom and beneficence of its chastisements, and men become reconciled to the agents through whom it operates, and have extolled them as heroes, benefactors and demigods.

To the broad vision of a true philosophy, nothing in this world stands alone. Everything is a necessary part of everything else. The margin of chance is narrowed by every extension of reason and knowledge, and nothing comes unbidden to the feast of human experience. The universe, of which we are a part, is continually proving itself a stupendous whole, a system of law and order, eternal and perfect. Every seed bears fruit after its kind, and nothing is reaped which was not sowed. The distance between seed time and harvest, in the moral world, may not be quite so well defined or as clearly intelligible as in the physical, but there is a seed time, and there is a harvest time, and though ages may intervene, and neither he who ploughed nor he who sowed may reap in person, yet the harvest nevertheless will surely come, and as in the physical world there are century plants, so it may be in the moral world, and their fruitage is as certain in the one as in the other. The bloody harvest of Harper's Ferry was ripened by the heat and moisture of merciless bondage of more than two hundred years. That startling cry of alarm on the banks of the Potomac was but the answering back of the avenging angel to the midnight invasions of Christian slave-traders on the sleeping hamlets of Africa. The history of the African slave-trade furnishes many illustrations far more cruel and bloody.

Viewed thus broadly our subject is worthy of thoughtful and dispassionate consideration. It invites the study of the poet, scholar, philosopher and statesman. What the masters in natural science have done for man in the physical world, the masters of social science may yet do for him in the moral world. Science now tells us when storms are in the sky, and when and where their violence will be most felt. Why may we not yet know with equal certainty when storms are in the moral sky, and how to avoid their desolating force? But I can invite you to no such profound discussions. I am not the man, nor is this the occasion for such philosophical enquiry. Mine is the word of grateful memory to an old friend; to tell you what I knew of him—what I knew of his inner life—of what he did and what he attempted, and thus if possible to make the mainspring of his actions manifest and thereby give you a clearer view of his character and services.

It is said that next in value to the performance of great deeds ourselves, is the capacity to appreciate such when performed by others; to more than this I do not presume. Allow me one other personal word before I proceed. In the minds of some of the American people I was myself credited with an important agency in the John Brown raid. Governor Henry A. Wise was manifestly of that opinion. He was at the pains of having Mr. Buchanan send his Marshals to Rochester to invite me to accompany them to Virginia. Fortunately I left town several hours previous to their arrival.

What ground there was for this distinguished consideration shall duly appear in the natural course of this lecture. I wish however to say just here that there was no foundation whatever for the charge that I in any wise urged or instigated John Brown to his dangerous work. I rejoice that it is my good fortune to have seen, not only the end of slavery, but to see the day when the whole truth can be told about this matter without prejudice to either the living or the dead. I shall however allow myself little prominence in these disclosures. Your interests, like mine, are in the all-commanding figure of the story, and to him I consecrate the hour. His zeal in the cause of my race was far greater than mine—it was as the burning sun to my taper light—mine was bounded by time, his stretched away to the boundless shores of eternity. I could live for the slave, but he could die for him. The crown of martyrdom is high, far beyond the reach of ordinary mortals, and yet happily no special greatness or superior moral excellence is necessary to discern and in some measure appreciate a truly great soul. Cold, calculating and unspiritual as most of us are, we are not wholly insensible to real greatness; and when we are brought in contact with a man of commanding mold, towering high and alone above the millions, free from all conventional fetters, true to his own moral convictions, a "law unto himself," ready to suffer misconstruction, ignoring torture and death for what he believes to be right, we are compelled to do him homage.

In the stately shadow, in the sublime presence of such a soul I find myself standing to-night; and how to do it reverence, how to do it justice, how to honor the dead with due regard to the living, has been a matter of most anxious solicitude.

Much has been said of John Brown, much that is wise and beautiful, but in looking over what may be called the John Brown literature, I have been little assisted with material, and even less encouraged with any hope of success in treating the subject. Scholarship, genius and devotion have hastened with poetry and eloquence, story and song to this simple altar of

human virtue, and have retired dissatisfied and distressed with
the thinness and poverty of their offerings, as I shall with mine.

The difficulty in doing justice to the life and character of
such a man is not altogether due to the quality of the zeal, or
of the ability brought to the work, nor yet to any imperfections
in the qualities of the man himself; the state of the moral atmosphere about us has much to do with it. The fault is not in our
eyes, nor yet in the object, if under a murky sky we fail to
discover the object. Wonderfully tenacious is the taint of a great
wrong. The evil, as well as "the good that men do, lives after
them." Slavery is indeed gone; but its long, black shadow yet
falls broad and large over the face of the whole country. It is the
old truth oft repeated, and never more fitly than now, "a prophet
is without honor in his own country and among his own people."
Though more than twenty years have rolled between us and the
Harper's Ferry raid, though since then the armies of the nation
have found it necessary to do on a large scale what John Brown
attempted to do on a small one, and the great captain who
fought his way through slavery has filled with honor the
Presidential chair, we yet stand too near the days of slavery, and
the life and times of John Brown, to see clearly the true martyr
and hero that he was and rightly to estimate the value of the
man and his works. Like the great and good of all ages—the men
born in advance of their times, the men whose bleeding footprints attest the immense cost of reform, and show us the long
and dreary spaces, between the luminous points in the progress
of mankind,—this our noblest American hero must wait the
polishing wheels of after-coming centuries to make his glory
more manifest, and his worth more generally acknowledged.
Such instances are abundant and familiar. If we go back four
and twenty centuries, to the stately city of Athens, and search
among her architectural splendor and her miracles of art for the
Socrates of today, and as he stands in history, we shall find
ourselves perplexed and disappointed. In Jerusalem Jesus himself
was only the "carpenter's son"—a young man wonderfully

destitute of worldly prudence—a pestilent fellow, "inexcusably and perpetually interfering in the world's business,"—"upsetting the tables of the money-changers"—preaching sedition, opposing the good old religion—"making himself greater than Abraham," and at the same time "keeping company" with very low people; but behold the change! He was a great miracle-worker, in his day, but time has worked for him a greater miracle than all his miracles, for now his name stands for all that is desirable in government, noble in life, orderly and beautiful in society. That which time has done for other great men of his class, that will time certainly do for John Brown. The brightest gems shine at first with subdued light, and the strongest characters are subject to the same limitations. Under the influence of adverse education and hereditary bias, few things are more difficult than to render impartial justice. Men hold up their hands to Heaven, and swear they will do justice, but what are oaths against prejudice and against inclination! In the face of high-sounding professions and affirmations we know well how hard it is for a Turk to do justice to a Christian, or for a Christian to do justice to a Jew. How hard for an Englishman to do justice to an Irishman, for an Irishman to do justice to an Englishman, harder still for an American tainted by slavery to do justice to the Negro or the Negro's friends. "John Brown," said the late Wm. H. Seward, "was justly hanged." "John Brown," said the late John A. Andrew, "was right." It is easy to perceive the sources of these two opposite judgments: the one was the verdict of slaveholding and panic-stricken Virginia, the other was the verdict of the best heart and brain of free old Massachusetts. One was the heated judgment of the passing and passionate hour, and the other was the calm, clear, unimpeachable judgment of the broad, illimitable future.

There is, however, one aspect of the present subject quite worthy of notice, for it makes the hero of Harper's Ferry in some degree an exception to the general rules to which I have just now adverted. Despite the hold which slavery had at that time on the country, despite the popular prejudice against the Negro, despite the shock which the first alarm occasioned, almost from the first John Brown received a large measure of sympathy and appreciation. New England recognized in him the spirit which brought the pilgrims to Plymouth rock and hailed him as a martyr and saint. True he had broken the law, true he had struck for a despised people, true he had crept upon his foe stealthily, like a wolf upon the fold, and had dealt his blow in the dark whilst his enemy slept, but with all this and more to disturb the moral sense, men discerned in him the greatest and best qualities known to human nature, and pronounced him "good." Many consented to his death, and then went home and taught their children to sing his praise as one whose "soul is marching on" through the realms of endless bliss. One element in explanation of this somewhat anomalous circumstance will probably be found in the troubled times which immediately succeeded, for "when judgments are abroad in the world, men learn righteousness."

The country had before this learned the value of Brown's heroic character. He had shown boundless courage and skill in dealing with the enemies of liberty in Kansas. With men so few, and means so small, and odds against him so great, no captain ever surpassed him in achievements, some of which seem almost beyond belief. With only eight men in that bitter war, he met, fought and captured Henry Clay Pate, with twenty-five well armed and mounted men. In this memorable encounter, he selected his ground so wisely, handled his men so skillfully, and attacked the enemy so vigorously, that they could neither run nor fight, and were therefore compelled to surrender to a force less than one-third their own. With just thirty men on another important occasion during the same border war, he met and vanquished four hundred Missourians under the command of Gen. Read. These men had come into the territory under an oath never to return to their homes till they had stamped out the last vestige of free State spirit in Kansas; but a brush with old Brown took this high conceit out of them, and they were glad to get off upon any terms, without stopping to stipulate. With less than one hundred men to defend the town of Lawrence, he offered to lead them and give battle to fourteen hundred men on the banks of the Waukerusia [sic] river, and was much vexed when his offer was refused by Gen. Jim Lane and others to whom the defense of the town was confided. Before leaving Kansas, he went into the border of Missouri, and liberated a dozen slaves in a single night, and, in spite of slave laws and marshals, he brought these people through a half dozen States, and landed them safely in Canada. With eighteen men this man shook the whole social fabric of Virginia. With eighteen men he overpowered a town of nearly three thousand souls. With these eighteen men he held that large community firmly in his grasp for thirty long hours. With these eighteen men he rallied in a single night fifty slaves to his standard, and made prisoners of an equal number of the slaveholding class. With these eighteen men he defied the power and bravery of a dozen of the best militia companies that Virginia could send against him. Now, when slavery struck, as it certainly did strike, at the life of the country, it was not the fault of John Brown that our rulers did not at first know how to deal with it. He had already shown us the weak side of the rebellion, had shown us where to strike and how. It was not from lack of native courage that Virginia submitted for thirty long hours and at last was relieved only by Federal troops, but because the attack was made on the side of her conscience and thus armed her against herself. She beheld at her side the sullen brow of a black Ireland. When John Brown proclaimed emancipation to the slaves of Maryland and Virginia he added to his war power the force of a moral earthquake. Virginia felt all her strong-ribbed mountains to shake under the heavy tread of armed insurgents. Of his army of nineteen her conscience made an army of nineteen hundred.

Another feature of the times, worthy of notice, was the effect of this blow upon the country at large. At the first moment we were stunned and bewildered. Slavery had so benumbed the moral sense of the nation, that it never suspected the possibility of an explosion like this, and it was difficult for Captain Brown to get himself taken for what he really was. Few could seem to comprehend that freedom to the slaves was his only object. If you will go back with me to that time you will find that the most curious and contradictory versions of the affair were industriously circulated, and those which were the least rational and true seemed to command the readiest belief. In the view of some, it assumed tremendous proportions. To such it was nothing less than a wide-sweeping rebellion to overthrow the existing government, and construct another upon its ruins, with Brown for its President and Commander-in-Chief, the proof of this was found in the old man's carpet-bag in the shape of a constitution for a new Republic, an instrument which in reality had been executed to govern the conduct of his men in the mountains. Smaller and meaner natures saw in it nothing higher than a purpose to plunder. To them John Brown and his men were a gang of desperate robbers, who had learned by some means that the government had sent a large sum of money to Harper's Ferry to pay off the workmen in its employ there, and they had gone thence to fill their pockets from this money. The fact is, that outside of a few friends, scattered in different parts of the country, and the slaveholders of Virginia, few persons understood the significance of the hour. That a man might do something very audacious and desperate for money, power or fame, was to the general apprehension quite possible, but, in face of plainly-written law, in face of constitutional guarantees protecting each State against domestic violence, in face of a nation of forty million of people, that nineteen men could invade a great State to liberate a despised and hated race, was to the average intellect and conscience, too monstrous for belief. In this respect the vision of Virginia was clearer than that of the nation. Conscious of her guilt and therefore full of suspicion, sleeping on pistols for pillows, startled at every unusual sound,

constantly fearing and expecting a repetition of the Nat Turner
insurrection, she at once understood the meaning, if not the
magnitude of the affair. It was this understanding which caused
her to raise the lusty and imploring cry to the Federal Government
for help, and it was not till he who struck the blow had fully
explained his motives and object, that the incredulous nation
in any wise comprehended the true spirit of the raid, or of its
commander. Fortunate for his memory, fortunate for the brave
men associated with him, fortunate for the truth of history,
John Brown survived the saber gashes, bayonet wounds and
bullet holes, and was able, though covered with blood, to tell
his own story and make his own defense. Had he with all his
men, as might have been the case, gone down in the shock of
battle, the world would have had no true basis for its judgment,
and one of the most heroic efforts ever witnessed in behalf of
liberty would have been confounded with base and selfish purposes. When, like savages, the Wises, the Vallandinghams, the
Washingtons, the Stuarts and others stood around the fallen
and bleeding hero, and sought by torturing questions to wring
from his supposed dying lips some word by which to soil the
sublime undertaking, by implicating Gerrit Smith, Joshua R.
Giddings, Dr. S. G. Howe, G. L. Steams, Edwin Morton, Frank
Sanborn, and other prominent Anti-slavery men, the brave old
man, not only avowed his object to be the emancipation of the
slaves, but serenely and proudly announced himself as solely
responsible for all that had happened. Though some thought
of his own life might at such a moment have seemed natural
and excusable, he showed none, and scornfully rejected the idea
that he acted as the agent or instrument of any man or set of
men. He admitted that he had friends and sympathizers, but
to his own head he invited all the bolts of slaveholding wrath
and fury, and welcomed them to do their worst. His manly
courage and self-forgetful nobleness were not lost upon the
crowd about him, nor upon the country. They drew applause

from his bitterest enemies. Said Henry A. Wise, "He is the gamest man I ever met." "He was kind and humane to his prisoners," said Col. Lewis Washington.

To the outward eye of men, John Brown was a criminal, but to their inward eye he was a just man and true. His deeds might be disowned, but the spirit which made those deeds possible was worthy highest honor. It has been often asked, why did not Virginia spare the life of this man? why did she not avail herself of this grand opportunity to add to her other glory that of a lofty magnanimity? Had they spared the good old man's life— had they said to him, "You see we have you in our power, and could easily take your life, but we have no desire to hurt you in any way; you have committed a terrible crime against society; you have invaded us at midnight and attacked a sleeping community, but we recognize you as a fanatic, and in some sense instigated by others; and on this ground and others, we release you. Go about your business, and tell those who sent you that we can afford to be magnanimous to our enemies." I say, had Virginia held some such language as this to John Brown, she would have inflicted a heavy blow on the whole Northern abolition movement, one which only the omnipotence of truth and the force of truth could have overcome. I have no doubt Gov. Wise would have done so gladly, but, alas, he was the executive of a State which thought she could not afford such magnanimity. She had that within her bosom which could more safely tolerate the presence of a criminal than a saint, a highway robber than a moral hero. All her hills and valleys were studded with material for a disastrous conflagration, and one spark of the dauntless spirit of Brown might set the whole State in flames. A sense of this appalling liability put an end to every noble consideration. His death was a foregone conclusion, and his trial was simply one of form.

Honor to the brave young Col. Hoyt who hastened from Massachusetts to defend his friend's life at the peril of his own;

but there would have been no hope of success had he been allowed to plead the case. He might have surpassed Choate or Webster in power—a thousand physicians might have sworn that Capt. Brown was insane, it would have been all to no purpose, neither eloquence nor testimony could have prevailed. Slavery was the idol of Virginia, and pardon and life to Brown meant condemnation and death to slavery. He had practically illustrated a truth stranger than fiction,—a truth higher than Virginia had ever known,—a truth more noble and beautiful than Jefferson ever wrote. He had evinced a conception of the sacredness and value of liberty which transcended in sublimity that of her own Patrick Henry and made even his fire-flashing sentiment of "Liberty or Death" seem dark and tame and selfish. Henry loved liberty for himself, but this man loved liberty for all men, and for those most despised and scorned, as well as for those most esteemed and honored. Just here was the true glory of John Brown's mission. It was not for his own freedom that he was thus ready to lay down his life, for with Paul he could say, "I was born free." No chain had bound his ankle, no yoke had galled his neck. History has no better illustration of pure, disinterested benevolence. It was not Caucasian for Caucasian—white man for white man; not rich man for rich man, but Caucasian for Ethiopian—white man for black man— rich man for poor man—the man admitted and respected, for the man despised and rejected. "I want you to understand, gentlemen," he said to his persecutors, "that I respect the rights of the poorest and weakest of the colored people, oppressed by the slave system, as I do those of the most wealthy and powerful." In this we have the key to the whole life and career of the man. Than in this sentiment humanity has nothing more touching, reason nothing more noble, imagination nothing more sublime, and if we could reduce all the religions of the world to one essence we could find in it nothing more divine. It is much to be regretted that some great artist, in sympathy with the spirit of the occasion, had not been present when these and similar words were spoken. The situation was thrilling. An old man in the center of an excited and angry crowd, far away from home, in an enemy's country—with no friend near—overpowered, defeated, wounded, bleeding—covered with reproaches—his brave companions nearly all dead—his two faithful sons stark and cold by his side—reading his death-warrant in his fast-oozing blood and increasing weakness as in the faces of all around him—yet calm, collected, brave, with a heart for any fate—using his supposed dying moments to explain his course and vindicate his cause: such a subject would have been at once an inspiration and a power for one of the grandest historical pictures ever painted.

With John Brown, as with every other man fit to die for a cause, the hour of his physical weakness was the hour of his moral strength—the hour of his defeat was the hour of his triumph—the moment of his capture was the crowning victory of his life. With the Alleghany mountains for his pulpit, the country for his church and the whole civilized world for his audience, he was a thousand times more effective as a preacher than as a warrior, and the consciousness of this fact was the secret of his amazing complacency. Mighty with the sword of steel, he was mightier with the sword of the truth, and with this sword he literally swept the horizon. He was more than a match for all the Wises, Masons, Vallandinghams and Washingtons, who could rise against him. They could kill him, but they could not answer him.

In studying the character and works of a great man, it is always desirable to learn in what he is distinguished from others, and what have been the causes of this difference. Such men as he whom we are now considering, come on to the theater of life only at long intervals. It is not always easy to explain the exact and logical causes that produce them, or the subtle influences which sustain them, at the immense heights where we sometimes find them, but we know that the hour and the man are seldom far apart, and that here, as elsewhere, the demand may in some mysterious way, regulate the supply. A great iniquity, hoary with age, proud and defiant, tainting the whole moral atmosphere of the country, subjecting both church and state to its control, demanded the startling shock which John Brown seemed especially inspired to give it.

Apart from this mission there was nothing very remarkable about him. He was a wool-dealer, and a good judge of wool, as a wool-dealer ought to be. In all visible respects he was a man like unto other men. No outward sign of Kansas or Harper's Ferry was about him. As I knew him, he was an even-tempered man, neither morose, malicious nor misanthropic, but kind, amiable, courteous, and gentle in his intercourse with men. His words were few, well chosen and forcible. He was a good business man, and a good neighbor. A good friend, a good citizen, a good husband and father: a man apparently in every way calculated to make a smooth and pleasant path for himself through the world. He loved society, he loved little children, he liked music, and was fond of animals. To no one was the world more beautiful or life more sweet. How then as I have said shall we explain his apparent indifference to life? I can find but one answer, and that is, his intense hatred to oppression. I have talked with many men, but I remember none, who seemed so deeply excited upon the subject of slavery as he. He would walk the room in agitation at mention of the word. He saw the evil through no mist or haze, but in a light of infinite brightness, which left no line of its ten thousand horrors out of sight. Law, religion, learning, were interposed in its behalf in vain. His law in regard to it was that which Lord Brougham described, as "the law above all the enactments of human codes, the same in all time, the same throughout the world—the law unchangeable and eternal—the law written by the finger of God on the human heart—that law by which property in man is, and ever must remain, a wild and guilty phantasy."

Against truth and right, legislative enactments were to his mind mere cobwebs—the pompous emptiness of human pride—the pitiful outbreathings of human nothingness. He used to say "whenever there is a right thing to be done, there is a ''thus saith the Lord' that it shall be done."

It must be admitted that Brown assumed tremendous responsibility in making war upon the peaceful people of Harper's Ferry, but it must be remembered also that in his eye a slaveholding community could not be peaceable, but was, in the nature of the case, in one incessant state of war. To him such a community was not more sacred than a band of robbers: it was the right of any one to assault it by day or night. He saw no hope that slavery would ever be abolished by moral or political means: "he knew," he said, "the proud and hard hearts of the slaveholders, and that they never would consent to give up their slaves, till they felt a big stick about their heads." It was five years before this event at Harper's Ferry, while the conflict between freedom and slavery was waxing hotter and hotter with every hour, that the blundering statesmanship of the National Government repealed the Missouri compromise, and thus launched the territory of Kansas as a prize to be battled for between the North and the South. The remarkable part taken in this contest by Brown has been already referred to, and it doubtless helped to prepare him for the final tragedy, and though it did not by any means originate the plan, it confirmed him in it and hastened its execution.

During his four years' service in Kansas it was my good fortune to see him often. On his trips to and from the territory he sometimes stopped several days at my house, and at one time several weeks. It was on this last occasion that liberty had been victorious in Kansas, and he felt that he must hereafter devote himself to what he considered his larger work. It was the theme of all his conversation, filling his nights with dreams and his days with visions. An incident of his boyhood may explain, in some measure, the intense abhorrence he felt to slavery. He had for some reason been sent into the State of Kentucky, where he made the acquaintance of a slave boy, about his own age, of whom he became very fond. For some petty offense this boy was one day subjected to a brutal beating. The blows were dealt with an iron shovel and fell fast and furiously upon his slender body. Born in a free State and unaccustomed to such scenes of cruelty, young Brown's pure and sensitive soul revolted at the shocking spectacle and at that early age he swore eternal hatred to slavery. After years never obliterated the impression, and he found in this early experience an argument against contempt for small things. It is true that the boy is the father of the man. From the acorn comes the oak. The impression of a horse's foot in the sand suggested the art of printing. The fall of an apple intimated the law of gravitation. A word dropped in the woods of Vincennes, by royal hunters, gave Europe and the world a "William the Silent," and a thirty years' war. The beating of a Hebrew bondsman, by an Egyptian, created a Moses, and the infliction of a similar outrage on a helpless slave boy in our own land may have caused, forty years afterwards, a John Brown and a Harper's Ferry Raid.

Most of us can remember some event or incident which has at some time come to us, and made itself a permanent part of our lives. Such an incident came to me in the year 1847. I had then the honor of spending a day and a night under the roof of a man, whose character and conversation made a very deep impression on my mind and heart; and as the circumstance does not lie entirely out of the range of our present observations, you will pardon for a moment a seeming digression. The name of the person alluded to had been several times mentioned to me, in a tone that made me curious to see him and to make his acquaintance. He was a merchant, and our first meeting was at his store—a substantial brick building, giving evidence of a flourishing business. After a few minutes' detention here, long enough for me to observe the neatness and order of the place, I was conducted by him to his residence where I was kindly received by his family as an expected guest. I was a little disappointed at the appearance of this man's house, for after seeing his fine store, I was prepared to see a fine residence; but this logic was entirely contradicted by the facts. The house was a small, wooden one, on a back street in a neighborhood of laboring men and mechanics, respectable enough, but not just the spot where one would expect to find the home of a successful merchant. Plain as was the outside, the inside was plainer. Its furniture might have pleased a Spartan. It would take longer to tell what was not in it, than what was, no sofas, no cushions, no curtains, no carpets, no easy rocking chairs inviting to ener- vation or rest or repose. My first meal passed under the misnomer of tea. It was none of your tea and toast sort, but potatoes and cabbage, and beef soup, such a meal as a man might relish after following the plough all day, or after performing a forced march of a dozen miles over rough ground in frosty weather. Innocent of paint, veneering, varnish or tablecloth, the table announced itself unmistakably and honestly pine and of the plainest work- manship. No hired help passed from kitchen to dining room, staring in amazement at the colored man at the white man's table. The mother, daughters and sons did the serving, and did it well. I heard no apology for doing their own work; they went through it as if used to it, untouched by any thought of degra- dation or impropriety. Supper over, the boys helped to clear the table and wash the dishes. This style of housekeeping struck me as a little odd. I mention it because household management is worthy of thought. A house is more than brick and mortar, wood or paint, this to me at least was. In its plainness it was a truthful reflection of its inmates: no disguises, no illusions, no make-believes here, but stern truth and solid purpose breathed in all its arrangements. I was not long in company with the master of this house before I discovered that he was indeed the master of it, and likely to become mine too, if I staid long with him. He fulfilled St. Paul's idea of the head of the family— his wife believed in him, and his children observed him with reverence. Whenever he spoke, his words commanded earnest attention. His arguments which I ventured at some points to oppose, seemed to convince all, his appeals touched all, and his will impressed all. Certainly I never felt myself in the presence of a stronger religious influence than while in this house. "God and duty, God and duty," run like a thread of gold through all his utterances, and his family supplied a ready "Amen." In person he was lean and sinewy, of the best New England mould, built for times of trouble, fitted to grapple with the flintiest hardships. Clad in plain American woolen, shod in boots of cowhide leather, and wearing a cravat of the same substantial material, under six feet high, less than one hundred and fifty lbs. in weight, aged about fifty, he presented a figure straight and symmetrical as a mountain pine. His bearing was singularly impressive. His head was not large, but compact and high. His hair was coarse, strong, slightly gray and closely trimmed and grew close to his forehead. His face was smoothly shaved and revealed a strong square mouth, supported by a broad and prominent chin. His eyes were clear and grey, and in conversation they alternated with tears and fire. When on the street, he moved with a long springing, race-horse step, absorbed by his own reflections, neither seeking nor shunning observation. Such was the man whose name I heard uttered in whispers—such was the house in which he lived—such were his family and household management—and such was Captain John Brown. He said to me at this meeting, that he had invited me to his house for the especial purpose of laying before me his plan for the speedy emancipation of my race. He seemed to apprehend opposition on my part as he opened the subject and touched my vanity by saying, that he had observed my course at home and abroad, and wanted my cooperation. He said he had been for the last thirty years looking for colored men to whom he could safely reveal his secret, and had almost despaired, at times, of finding such, but that now he was encouraged for he saw heads rising up in all directions, to whom he thought he could with safety impart his plan. As this plan then lay in his mind it was very simple, and had much to commend it. It did not, as was supposed by many, contemplate a general rising among the slaves, and a general slaughter of the slave masters (an insurrection he thought would only defeat the object), but it did contemplate the creating of an armed force which should act in the very heart of the South. He was not averse to the shedding of blood, and thought the practice of carrying arms would be a good one for the colored people to adopt, as it would give them a sense of manhood. No people he said could have self-respect or be respected who would not fight for their freedom. He called my attention to a large map of the U. States, and pointed out to me the far-reaching Alleghenies, stretching away from the borders of New York into the Southern States. "These mountains," he said, "are the basis of my plan. God has given the strength of these hills to freedom, they were placed here to aid the emancipation of your race; they are full of natural forts, where one man for defense would be equal to a hundred for attack; they are also full of good hiding places where a large number of men could be concealed and baffle and elude pursuit for a long time. I know these mountains well and could take a body of men into them and keep them there in spite of all the efforts of Virginia to dislodge me, and drive me out. I would take at first about twenty-five picked men and begin on a small scale, supply them arms and ammunition, post them in squads of fives on a line of twenty-five miles, these squads to busy themselves for a time in gathering recruits from the surrounding farms, seeking and selecting the most restless and daring." He saw that in this part of the work the utmost care must be used to guard against treachery and disclosure; only the most conscientious and skillful should be sent on this perilous duty. With care and enterprise he thought he could soon gather a force of one hundred hardy men, men who would be content to lead the free and adventurous life to which he proposed to train them. When once properly drilled and each had found the place for which he was best suited, they would begin work in earnest; they would run off the slaves in large numbers, retain the strong and brave ones in the mountains, and send the weak and timid ones to the North by the underground railroad, his operations would be enlarged with increasing numbers and would not be confined to one locality. Slaveholders should in some cases be approached at midnight and told to give up their slaves and to let them have their best horses to ride away upon. Slavery was a state of war, he said, to which the slaves were unwilling parties and consequently they had a right to anything necessary to their peace and freedom. He would shed no blood and would avoid a fight except in self-defense, when he would of course do his best. He believed this movement would weaken slavery in two ways—first by making slave property insecure, it would become undesirable; and secondly it would keep the anti-slavery agitation alive and public attention fixed upon it, and thus lead to the adoption of measures to abolish the evil altogether. He held that there was need of something startling to prevent the agitation of the question from dying out; that slavery had come near being abolished in Virginia by the Nat Turner insurrection, and he thought his method would speedily put an end to it, both in Maryland and Virginia. The trouble was to get the right men to start with and money enough to equip them. He had adopted the simple and economical mode of living to which I have referred with a view to save money for this purpose. This was said in no boastful tone, for he felt that he had delayed already too long and had no room to boast either his zeal or his self-denial.

From 8 o'clock in the evening till 3 in the morning, Capt. Brown and I sat face to face, he arguing in favor of his plan, and I finding all the objections I could against it. Now mark! this meeting of ours was full twelve years before the strike at Harper's Ferry. He had been watching and waiting all that time for suitable heads to rise or "pop up" as he said among the sable millions in whom he could confide; hence forty years had passed between his thought and his act. Forty years, though not a long time in the life of a nation, is a long time in the life of a man; and here forty long years, this man was struggling with this one idea; like Moses he was forty years in the wilderness. Youth, manhood, middle age had come and gone; two marriages had been consummated, twenty children had called him father; and through all the storms and vicissitudes of busy life, this one thought, like the angel in the burning bush, had confronted him with its blazing light, bidding him on to his work. Like Moses he had made excuses, and as with Moses his excuses were overruled. Nothing should postpone further what was to him a divine command, the performance of which seemed to him his only apology for existence. He often said to me, though life was sweet to him, he would willingly lay it down for the freedom of my people; and on one occasion he added, that he had already lived about as long as most men, since he had slept less, and if he should now lay down his life the loss would not be great, for in fact he knew no better use for it. During his last visit to us in Rochester there appeared in the newspapers a touching story connected with the horrors of the Sepoy War in British India. A Scotch missionary and his family were in the hands of the enemy, and were to be massacred the next morning. During the night, when they had given up every hope of rescue, suddenly the wife insisted that relief would come. Placing her ear close to the ground she declared she heard the Slogan—the Scotch war song. For long hours in the night no member of the family could hear the advancing music but herself. "Dinna ye hear it? Dinna ye hear it?" she would say, but they could not hear it. As the morning slowly dawned a Scotch regiment was found encamped indeed about them, and they were saved from the threatened slaughter. This circumstance, coming at such a time, gave Capt. Brown a new word of cheer. He would come to the table in the morning his countenance fairly illuminated, saying that he had heard the Slogan, and he would add, "Dinna ye hear it? Dinna ye hear it?" Alas! like the Scotch missionary I was obliged to say "No." Two weeks prior to the meditated attack, Capt. Brown summoned me to meet him in an old stone quarry on the Conecochequi river, near the town of Chambersburgh, Penn. His arms and ammunition were stored in that town and were to be moved on to Harper's Ferry. In company with Shields Green I obeyed the summons, and prompt to the hour we met the dear old man, with Kagi, his secretary, at the appointed place. Our meeting was in some sense a council of war. We spent the Saturday and succeeding Sunday in conference on the question, whether the desperate step should then be taken, or the old plan as already described should be carried out. He was for boldly striking Harper's Ferry at once and running the risk of getting into the mountains afterwards. I was for avoiding Harper's Ferry altogether. Shields Green and Mr. Kagi remained silent listeners throughout. It is needless to repeat here what was said, after what has happened. Suffice it, that after all I could say, I saw that my old friend had resolved on his course and that it was idle to parley. I told him finally that it was impossible for me to join him. I could see Harper's Ferry only as a trap of steel, and ourselves in the wrong side of it. He regretted my decision and we parted.

Thus far, I have spoken exclusively of Capt. Brown. Let me say a word or two of his brave and devoted men, and first of Shields Green. He was a fugitive slave from Charleston, South Carolina, and had attested his love of liberty by escaping from slavery and making his way through many dangers to Rochester, where he had lived in my family, and where he met the man with whom he went to the scaffold. I said to him, as I was about to leave, "Now Shields, you have heard our discussion. If in view of it, you do not wish to stay, you have but to say so, and you can go back with me." He answered, "I b'l'eve I'll go wid de old man;" and go with him he did, into the fight, and to the gallows, and bore himself as grandly as any of the number. At the moment when Capt. Brown was surrounded, and all chance of escape was cut off, Green was in the mountains and could have made his escape as Osborne Anderson did, but when asked to do so, he made the same answer he did at Chambersburg, "I b'l'eve I'll go down wid de ole man." When in prison at Charlestown, and he was not allowed to see his old friend, his fidelity to him was in no wise weakened, and no complaint against Brown could be extorted from him by those who talked with him.

If a monument should be erected to the memory of John Brown, as there ought to be, the form and name of Shields Green should have a conspicuous place upon it. It is a remarkable fact, that in this small company of men, but one showed any sign of weakness or regret for what he did or attempted to do. Poor Cook broke down and sought to save his life by representing that he had been deceived, and allured by false promises. But Stephens, Hazlett and Green went to their doom like the heroes they were, without a murmur, without a regret, believing alike in their captain and their cause.

For the disastrous termination of this invasion, several causes have been assigned. It has been said that Capt. Brown found it necessary to strike before he was ready; that men had promised to join him from the North who failed to arrive; that the cowardly Negroes did not rally to his support as he expected, but the true cause as stated by himself, contradicts all these theories, and from his statement there is no appeal. Among the questions put to him by Mr. Vallandingham after his capture were the following: "Did you expect a general uprising of the slaves in case of your success?" To this he answered, "No, sir, nor did I wish it. I expected to gather strength from time to time and then to set them free." "Did you expect to hold possession here until then?" Answer, "Well, probably I had quite a different idea. I do not know as I ought to reveal my plans. I am here wounded and a prisoner because I foolishly permitted myself to be so. You overstate your strength when you suppose I could have been taken if I had not allowed it. I was too tardy after commencing the open attack in delaying my movements through Monday night and up to the time of the arrival of government troops. It was all because of my desire to spare the feelings of my prisoners and their families."

But the question is, Did John Brown fail? He certainly did fail to get out of Harper's Ferry before being beaten down by

United States soldiers; he did fail to save his own life, and to lead a liberating army into the mountains of Virginia. But he did not go to Harper's Ferry to save his life. The true question is, Did John Brown draw his sword against slavery and thereby lose his life in vain? and to this I answer ten thousand times. No! No man fails, or can fail who so grandly gives himself and all he has to a righteous cause. No man, who in his hour of extremest need, when on his way to meet an ignominious death, could so forget himself as to stop and kiss a little child, one of the hated race for whom he was about to die, could by any possibility fail. Did John Brown fail? Ask Henry A. Wise in whose house less than two years after, a school for the emancipated slaves was taught. Did John Brown fail? Ask James M. Mason, the author of the inhuman fugitive slave bill, who was cooped up in Fort Warren, as a traitor less than two years from the time that he stood over the prostrate body of John Brown. Did John Brown fail? Ask Clement C. Vallandingham, one other of the inquisitorial party; for he too went down in the tremendous whirlpool created by the powerful hand of this bold invader. If John Brown did not end the war that ended slavery, he did at least begin the war that ended slavery. If we look over the dates, places and men, for which this honor is claimed, we shall find that not Carolina, but Virginia—not Fort Sumpter, but Harper's Ferry and the arsenal—not Col. Anderson, but John Brown, began the war that ended American slavery and made this a free Republic. Until this blow was struck, the prospect for freedom was dim, shadowy and uncertain. The irrepressible conflict was one of words, votes and compromises. When John Brown stretched forth his arm the sky was cleared. The time for compromises was gone—the armed hosts of freedom stood face to face over the chasm of a broken Union—and the clash of arms was at hand. The South staked all upon getting possession of the Federal Government, and failing to do that, drew the sword of rebellion and thus made her own, and not Brown's, the lost cause of the century.

THE RACE PROBLEM
(1890)

This address serves primarily as Douglass's reaction to the attempts of southern Resurrectionists to limit African American's newly won civil rights, placing the responsibility of protecting those rights firmly in the hands of the Federal Government. It was delivered before the Bethel Literary and Historical Association on October 21, 1890, at the Metropolitan A.M.E. Church in Washington, D.C.

MEMBERS AND FRIENDS of the Bethel Literary and Historical Association: I esteem it a great privilege to be with you and assist in this your first meeting since the close of your last winter's term. The organization of your association was an important step in the progress of the colored people in this city. It is an institution well fitted to improve the minds and elevate the sentiments not only of its members, but of the general public. Nowhere else outside of the courts of law and the Congress of the United States have I heard vital public questions more seriously discussed. The men selected to address you know very well that what they may utter is subjected to close scrutiny and severe discussion. Mere rant, bombast, and self-inflation may pass elsewhere, but not here. For this reason, and for my own self-respect, I shall endeavor to say only what I believe to be the truth upon what is popularly called "The Negro Problem."

My first thought respects the importance of calling things by their true names. This importance cannot be over-estimated or over-stated. Truth is the fundamental, indispensable, and everlasting requirement in obtaining right results. No department of human life can afford to dispense with truth. The carpenter cannot join his timbers without having the parts of contact perfectly true to each other. The mason cannot build a wall that will stand the test of time and gravitation without applying the plumb and making the wall vertical and true. No train or car is safe on the road where the relations of the rails are not true. No shot is certain of its aim where the gun-barrel is not true. As in mechanics, so in politics, morals, manners, metaphysics, and philosophies, nothing can stand the test of time and experience that does not stand on the unassailable, indestructible, unchangeable, foundation of truth. Considering how important this truth is, it seems strange that falsehood should hold such sway in the world. One main advantage by which error is able to darken, blight, and dominate the minds of men is the skill of its votaries in using language deceitfully, in pandering to prejudice by misstating and misapplying terms to the existing relations of men. It has been well said that in an important sense words are things. They are especially such when they are employed to express the popular sentiment concerning the Negro: to couple his name with anything in this world seems to damage it and damage him likewise. Hence I object to characterizing the relation subsisting between the white and colored people of this country as the Negro problem, as if the Negro had precipitated that problem, and as if he were in any way responsible for the problem. Though a rose by any other name may smell as sweet, it is not in good taste to give it a name that suggests offensive associations. There are, on the other hand, things that are in themselves revolting, and should not be given fair-seeming names. The slaveholders understood this principle well enough. Slavery lost something of its offensive aspect when it was called a domestic institution or a social system and other like names. Emancipation was made to look dangerous when it got itself called an experiment, although slavery itself was an experiment, and liberty is the normal condition of man. "The Negroes were the cause of the war," said Mr. Lincoln, and straightway the loyal soldiers of the Republic began to kick and beat the poor Negroes on the banks of the Potomac, and the Irish began to hang, stab, and murder the Negroes in New York. It is dangerous even to a dog to be given a bad name. I am, therefore, in favor of employing the truest and most agreeable names to describe the relation which at present subsists between ourselves and the other people of the country.

Again, another advantage to error, and one which is often employed with marked skill and effect, is the presentation to the minds of men of what may be called half truths for whole truths, and thus making a sweet and wholesome truth t' e cover for a bitter falsehood. A counterfeit nearest in likeness o what is genuine is always most likely to impose upon the unskillful. A lie ceases to be very dangerous when it parts with its ability to deceive. The devil is less dangerous as a roaring lion than when transformed as an angel of light.

The application of these homely truths and familiar examples will become apparent in the discussion I propose of what is popularly but improperly called the race problem. It seems that the American people have a special liking for this mathematical formula as applied to the Negro. They seem determined to keep his brain forever employed and his time forever occupied in solving a great variety of problems, and generally to his disadvantage. As soon as he solves one another is propounded to him, and when he thinks, good, easy soul, his work is done he finds a new one invented, a new burden imposed, and a new hardship inflicted. There may be rest for the weary, but there seems at present no rest for the Negro. He has been solving problems during all his history.

I have before referred in this place, I think, to the fact that the Negro was confronted 200 years ago by what was considered a great religious problem, one which was very difficult of solution. That problem was: Ought the Negro to be baptized in water and admitted to membership in the Christian church? This was, as I have often said, considering the time of it, a tremendous problem. As in our day in regard to Negro problems, the opinions of the wise and great were strongly pronounced and much divided. The right of the Negro to baptism was fiercely disputed, especially by those who owned them as slaves. What is plain to all now was dark and doubtful to many then. It is easy to fancy that men spoke of it with bated breath, and saw in the Negro's baptism a menace to the peace and stability of society, as well as of slavery. For to baptize the Negro and admit him to membership in the Christian church was to recognize him as a man, a child of God, an heir of Heaven, redeemed by the blood of Christ, a temple of the Holy Ghost, a standing type and representative of the Savior of the world, one who, according to the apostle Paul, must be treated no longer as a servant, but as a brother beloved. Viewed in this light, his admission to baptism, and to the church was a matter for the gravest consideration. It touched the money nerve of the Christians of that day, for their wealth was largely invested in Negro flesh and blood. It was well said that the proposition was novel, extraordinary, and full of danger. It would impair the value of the slave, and it would put in jeopardy the authority of the master: they were right, and if the Negro is to be regarded as a Christian, he could not be regarded as a heathen, and as the Bible sanctioned only the enslavement of heathen, the Negro Christian could not be bought and sold, enslaved and whipped, according to the requirements of the relation of master and slave. From every view they could then take of the proposition to baptize the Negro was rank radicalism and deserved stern resistance at its inception.

To the credit of the church and its ministers, it must be said that one learned and able divine, in the person of Dr. Godwin, was equal to the situation. He met the arguments of the opposition to Negro baptism in a book of 200 pages, in which he endeavored to show that baptism would not impair either the

value of the slave or the authority of the master. His argument
was a curious one. It divided the Negro into two separate parts,
giving one to the Lord and the other to the slaveholder, and
leaving nothing whatever of soul, body or spirit to himself.
Baptism, he said, freed the Negro from the bondage of the devil,
but not from the bondage of his earthly master. The controversy
over this problem was long and furious, and the Negro only
won a partial victory after all. The matter was finally settled,
as usual, by a kind of compromise. The Negro was baptized and
admitted to the church, but a sort of second table was set for
him. He could take the Lord's supper only after his white brethren had finished eating the bread and drinking the wine. He
was not even allowed to enter the same door of the sanctuary
by which his white brethren entered. A separate door was cut
for him in the wall, a sort of hole in the wall, leading to a high
and dark place in the gallery, where his presence could give no
offense to the Lord's white children on the floor.

It is strange that this state of things did not disgust and repel
the Negro, make him an infidel, and drive him from religion
altogether, but it did not. He clung to religion all the same.
Believing that half a loaf was better than no bread, he took what
he could get of the church, kept on praying and singing, and
sometimes shouting. He could pray as fervently for the conversion of the scoundrel who tore his flesh with the lash, as for his
best friend. He was made to think that his offensive black skin
on earth would be changed for a white one in Heaven. It was a
strange fancy, but quite a natural one when we see the importance given to color in the problems before us in our day.

Another problem greatly disturbed the conscientious during
the time of slavery. It was this: Can a Negro contract a valid
marriage? If he could, and could enforce his right to his wife
and children, it would prove an inconvenient limitation on the
power of his master. If what God has joined together no man
shall put asunder, the right to sell the wife from the husband
and the husband from the wife must cease. In the minds of the

men who had to deal with it no such limitation in the right of the master could be allowed or tolerated for a moment. The master must have the right to buy and sell as he pleased, was the solution of that problem. One terrible evil of this solution of the marriage question is still seen in our land. Unable to contract valid marriage, the Negro felt himself unrestrained, and licensed to do as he pleased. He was not expected to limit his conduct by any rule or principle of morality or decency, but took to himself the freedom of the beasts of the field and the fowls of the air. He had in law no wife, no family, no children, and did not own himself. The consequence of this state of things may be seen very often in our own city at the police court and elsewhere, and the strange thing is, the very people who are responsible for this immorality and crime make merry over our wretchedness and talk solemnly about the terrible Negro problem.

Happily for us, and happily for our common country, as we shall see later on, the Southern solution of this Negro problem has now been unsolved by the act of emancipation and the superior civilization of the loyal American people over the people of the old slaveholding States.

Another troublesome problem presented to our Christian country was whether the Negro should have the help of the Bible with which to get to Heaven; whether, in fact, the command to search the Scriptures imposed any obligation or duty on him. Our Southern brethren, with whom we have always been profoundly sympathetic even unto this day, decided this problem against the Bible, and against the Negro, as usual. They made it a crime, to be punished with banishment, imprisonment, and stripes, for any one to teach the Negro to read. Yet the descendants of these same men, with the education of their fathers, and with the antecedents of their fathers, are now asking us in piteous tones to allow them in their superior wisdom and goodness of heart to solve what they are pleased to call the Negro problem of today. They are crying out lustily to the nation, like demons tormented before their time, "Hands off! We want no Federal authority, and want only local self-government. We want to be let alone!" They tell us that they know the Negro, and that they can manage him better than anybody else. They can manage his wages, his voting, and his education, and all that pertains to him. I hope the nation will not let them do any such thing. They have shown a strange inaptitude for such a task. The point with them is not what is right, but what will best suit themselves.

But again, in the history of the Negro we had another perplexing problem. It was this, and this was in some sense a national problem: Can the Negro be made a soldier? This, too, was very serious problem for the country, for it was a matter of Union or no Union, of life or death. For at one time it needed all the material which the nation could command to settle the problem of our national existence. It will be remembered that at the beginning of the war it was given out that no Negro need apply. He was not to be allowed to shoulder a musket, carry a knapsack, or wear a Union uniform. The glory of the battlefield was to be won wholly by white men. The Negro might dig but not fight. He might be a servant, but not a soldier. He might carry a pick-ax, but never a musket.

In considering this problem the nation, strangely enough, shut its eyes to the fact that in the history of the Revolution the Negro fought bravely for American independence, and in the war of 1812 he even extorted praise for his valor from the stern lips of General Andrew Jackson. His fighting qualities were nobly admitted by the hero of New Orleans. In spite of this it was insisted that the Negro was a born coward that could never make a soldier: that he would run at the sight of a gun. Time and events however helped the Negro and the Nation in the solution of this problem, as I think they will help in the solution of any others that may arise. Fort Wagner, Port Hudson,

Vicksburg, James Island, Olustee, Petersburg, Richmond—a cloud of witnesses rise before us to solve the problem of the Negro's soldierly qualities.

Whether the Negro could be educated, was another problem, and I think this has been solved to the satisfaction of all candid men. He would be a dishonest man, or an amazingly stupid one who, in the face of the thousands of Negro teachers, the hundreds of Negro preachers, doctors, lawyers, authors, and editors, with which the country is now studded, should insist, as it was once insisted, that education was impossible to the Negro.

But the greatest problem for the Negro was whether he could with safety be made free. Good men knew that slavery was wrong, but how to get rid of it was the great question. Neither the pulpit, nor the press, nor the statesman could see a solution of the great problem, and yet that problem has been solved. The Negro is free, and the country is cleansed of its greatest curse, crime, and scandal.

There were terrible things to happen upon the passing away of slavery. The freedom of the slave was the signal of ruin. There was to be no more cotton, no more sugar, no more work done by the Negro, and the South was to become a howling wilderness. But against all these dark forebodings, these pictures of dismal terror, the late war made short work of the whole problem. That sturdy old Roman, Benjamin Butler, made the Negro a contraband, Abraham Lincoln made him a free man, and General Ulysses S. Grant made him a citizen, and not one of these terrible things have happened.

But now, though all this has been done, though slavery has been abolished, though the Negro has been freed, though he has become a citizen, though the Union has been saved, in part by his valor, the Negro is not to be let off quite yet. He is to be made the victim of a new deal by precipitating upon the country a false issue. He is to face another problem.

Now that the Union is no longer in danger, now that the North and South are no longer enemies: now that they have ceased to scatter, tear, and slay each other, but sit together in halls of Congress, commerce, religion, and in brotherly love, it seems that the Negro is to lose by their sectional harmony and good will all the rights and privileges that he gained by their former bitter enmity.

This, it is found, cannot be accomplished without confusing the moral sense of the nation and misleading the public mind; without creating doubt, inflaming passion, arousing prejudice, and attracting to the enemies of the Negro the popular sympathy by representing the Negro as an ignorant, base, and dangerous person, and by presenting to those enemies that his existence to them is a dreadful problem. With their usual cunning, these enemies of the Negro have made the North partly believe that they are now contending with a vast and mysterious problem, the mere contemplation of which should cause the whole North to shudder and come to the rescue. The trick is worthy of its inventors, and has been played for all that it is worth. The orators of the South have gone North and have eloquently described this terrible problem, and the press of the South has flamed with it, and grave Senators from that section have painted it in most distressing colors. Problem, problem, race problem, Negro problem, has, as Junius says, flitted through their sentences in all the mazes of metaphorical confusion.

In speaking of this subject in another place, I said what I say now, that these Southern people have outwitted the North in this problem business. Like skillful prestidigitators, they have turned the attention of the spectator to a distant object while they have manipulated the thing in hand. They imitated the cunning of the hunter who draws a red herring across the path of the game to divert the hounds.

The true problem is not the Negro, but the nation. Not the law-abiding blacks of the South, but the white men of that section, who by fraud, violence, and persecution, are breaking the law, trampling on the Constitution, corrupting the ballot-box, and defeating the ends of justice. The true problem is whether these white ruffians shall be allowed by the nation to go on in their lawless and nefarious career, dishonoring the Government and making its very name a mockery. It is whether this nation has in itself sufficient moral stamina to maintain its own honor and integrity by vindicating its own Constitution and fulfilling its own pledges, or whether it has already touched that dry rot of moral depravity by which nations decline and fall, and governments fade and vanish. The United States Government made the Negro a citizen; will it protect him as a citizen? This is the problem. It made him a soldier; will it honor him as a patriot? This is the problem. It made him a voter; will it defend his right to vote? This is the problem. This, I say, is more a problem for the nation than for the Negro, and this is the side of the question far more than the other, which should be kept in view by the American people.

What these problem orators now ask is that the nation shall undo all that it did by the suppression of the rebellion and in maintenance of the Union. They ask that the nation shall recede from its advance in the path of justice, liberty, and civilization. They boldly ask that what was justly and gratefully given to the Negro in the hour of national peril shall be taken from him in the hour of national security. They ask that the nation shall stultify itself and commit an act of national shame which ought to make every lover of his country cry out in bitter indignation and unite as one man to oppose. A demand so scandalous and so shocking to every sentiment of honor and gratitude.

And from whom does this demand come? Not from the men who gave their lives to save the nation, but from those who gave their lives to destroy it. Not from the free and loyal North, but from the rebellious and slaveholding South. Not from the section where men go to the ballot-box with the same freedom from personal danger as they go to church on Sunday, but from that section where personal safety is endangered, where Federal authority is defied, where the amendments to the Constitution are nullified, where the ballot-box is tainted by fraud, and red-shirted intimidation makes a free vote impossible. It comes from the men who led the nation in a dance of blood during four long years, and who now have the impudence to assume to control the destiny of this Republic as well as the destiny of the Negro.

And what are the reasons they give for demanding of the nation this retreat from its advanced position? They are these: They tell us that they are afraid, very much afraid; they are alarmed, very much alarmed, by the possibility of Negro supremacy over them. This is the calamity from which they would be delivered, and with eloquent lips and lusty lungs they are calling out: "Men and brethren, save us from this threatened and terrible danger!"

My reply to this alarm is easy. It is that the wicked flee when no man pursueth; that the thief thinks each bush an officer; that the thing they pretend to fear can never happen, and that blank absurdity is written upon the face of it. The eagle, with fierce talon and bloody beak screaming in terror at the approach of a harmless black bird would not be more absurd and ridiculous. The superior intelligence of the whites, the comparative ignorance of the blacks, the former dominion of the whites and the former subjection of the blacks, the habit of bearing rule of the whites, and the habit of submission by the blacks make black supremacy in any part of our common country utterly impossible.

But supposing such an occurrence possible, what hardship would it impose? What wrong would it inflict? Who would be injured by it? If the blacks should get the upper hand, their rule would have to be regulated by the Constitution and the laws of the United States. They could not discriminate against white people on account of race, color, or previous condition without finding the iron hand of the nation laid heavily on their shoulders. The white people of the South are the rich, the Negroes the poor; the white people are the landowners, the Negroes are the landless. The white people of the South are numbered with the ruling class of the nation. They have behind them every possible source of power. They have railroads, steamships, electric telegraphs, the Army and the Navy. They have the sword and the purse of the nation behind them, and yet they profess to be shaking in their shoes lest the 8,000,000 of blacks shall come to rule over them and their brethren, the 50,000,000 of whites.

Now I am here to say that there is nothing whatever in this supposition. I can hardly call this invention a cunning device, for the pretense is too open, too transparent, too absurd, to rise even to the dignity of low cunning. It is an old ragged pair of trousers, and an old mashed and battered hat of the last century stuck upon a pole in a field where there are neither crows nor corn. It is the cry of fire by the thief when he would divert the officer of the law. It is as I have said, a red herring to divert the hounds from the true game, and the strange thing is that any class of our citizens, white or black, can be deceived by it.

But black supremacy is not the only string on the harp of a thousand strings upon which our Southern brethren play. They are not merely afraid of black supremacy, but they are afraid of ignorant black supremacy. Now, this danger is just the one to appeal to the sympathy of the North. The Northern people are not in love with ignorance or illiteracy. They deplore it; they hate it, and take every means in their power to banish it from their States. They naturally sympathize with any people in deploring it and who are making honest efforts to remove it from among them. Hence they are pouring out millions of dollars to aid the South, and are sending competent teachers there to enlighten the ignorant and to lift up the black man and white man alike from the darkness and ignorance to which they had been doomed by slavery and by those would-be Negro problem solvers.

But it is worthy of emphatic remark that the men in the South who are loudest in their outcry against the ignorance of the Negro are not those who wish to have him instructed, but those who would make his ignorance a reason for depriving him of the rights secured to him under the Constitution.

But again, when before in the history of the Southern people have they been alarmed by the presence of ignorance among them? When before did they ask the nation to assist them in stemming the tide of ignorance? The whole history of the legislation of the South—by the South I mean the ruling class of the South—is on the side of ignorance. Their laws have made it a crime to enlighten the black man's ignorance. It has been the policy of the ruling class there to oppose education not only for the blacks, but for the poor whites as well. But as I have said, this cry is raised not for help to educate the Negro, but as an excuse for taking from him the right of suffrage, by which he can in some measure promote his own education and the education of those about him.

But admitting what I do not admit, that the ignorance of the Negro is recognized by the South as a source of danger, and admitting the sincerity of Southern men who are professing to deplore it, I have to say to them: If you could stand the Negro when he was a slave, you can stand it now that he is free, at least a reasonable length of time for his education. Clearly enough, the remedy is not in the abridgement of his rights, but in the education of his mind. It is not in evading the plain provisions of the Constitution, but in teaching him the duties imposed by the Constitution; not in taking away his vote, but in teaching him how to use it.

To me there is something very audacious and insolent rather than pathetic and persuasive in the language employed by Southern men on this question. There is something of the old-time Southern swagger and assumption in their tone and bearing—a tone and bearing which is entirely out of date, out of place, and out of harmony with the age and body of our time—a tone and bearing which invites rebuke rather than sympathy, disgust rather than approbation.

Such men as Senator Butler, of South Carolina, should remember that there is such a thing as modesty as well as decency for men of such antecedents as theirs and that it is neither modest nor decent for them to coolly propose the expulsion of citizens innocent of crime from the State of South Carolina, or from any other State in the American Union. It is only a little while ago that Senator Butler and his class were in arms against the Government which these same Negro citizens loyally and bravely endeavored to save from their disloyal hands.

But let me say again, the South neither really fears the ignorance of the Negro, nor the supremacy of the Negro. It is not the ignorant Negro, but the intelligent North that it fears; not the supremacy of a different race from itself, but the supremacy of the Republican party. It is not the men who are emancipated but the people who emancipated them that disturb its repose. In other words the trouble is not racial, but political. It is not the race and color of the vote. Disguise this as it may, the real thing that troubles the South is the Republican party, its principles, and its ascendancy in Southern States and the nation. When it talks of Negro ignorance, Negro supremacy, it means this, and simply this, only this. It uses the word Negro simply as a means to the end of awakening popular prejudice and enlisting its influence in favor of its bad cause, a cause for which they have shown themselves capable of committing every description of frauds the most scandalous, and cruelty the most barbarous. We all know that the Negro problem would vanish into thin air, would utterly disappear like the mist before the morning sun, if the intelligent Negroes of the South would renounce their connection with the Republican party and support only the Democratic party. What the South wants, and what it means to have peaceably if it can, or forcibly if it must, is a solid Democratic party South and Democratic rule in the nation. There is not an intelligent man at the South that does not know this, and there is not an honest man at the South, who, if he would speak candidly on the subject, would deny this. The trouble is that the people of the North do not see this in its true light. Honest themselves, they cannot readily believe that others are not alike honest. It is in some sense creditable in them that they have never believed in the story of outrages committed against the Negro voters of the South, because they themselves would not be guilty of such outrages, they have been easily imposed upon by the pretended fear of a Negro supremacy professed by the South.

But let me be more intelligible. My idea about the problem business is this: When a case has been in litigation before a court of highest resort, and that case has been solemnly adjudicated in that court, that case is finished and all the parties to it must submit to the decision or become law-breakers and criminals. The case goes into history hence forth *res adjudicata*. It is settled. If this beneficent rule did not exist there would be no end to litigation and no repose for the public mind.

To make my meaning still more clear: When in England a few years ago Northampton saw it fit to send Mr. Bradlaugh, an infidel, to represent it in the British House of Commons, and he was not allowed to take his seat, the admission of an infidel to the House of Commons was a problem; but when he continued to knock at the door of the House till he was finally admitted the infidel problem, so far as the right of membership of that House was concerned, was solved.

Again, we are not the only people whose rights have been denied on the ground of race. Our brother Shem has had a taste of proscription as well as ourselves. No Jew was at one time eligible to membership in the parliament of Great Britain, but after long years of agitation of the question, Mr. Baring, an eminent Jew, was admitted to a seat in parliament. The Jewish problem, when Mr. Baring was seated, was ended, I mean this: When the American people declared their independence of Great Britain and made good that declaration by victory in a seven years war, the problem of American independence was solved, and there was never anything afterwards concerning it which could be called problematical. It was a fixed fact, and has remained such until now, and will remain so, I trust, forever.

There is a grand agitation now in progress in Great Britain for local self-government, at the head of which are Mr. Gladstone and Mr. Parnell. If Great Britain shall grant home rule to Ireland, the Irish problem will be solved, and it will be nonsense thereafter to speak of it as an unsolved problem. Our American women are asking for a sixteenth amendment to the Constitution, whereby they may vote. They ought to have it. If the American people shall adopt such an amendment, the women problem will cease to exist.

In like manner, when the Negro was declared free by the highest authority in the land, when the whole system of his bondage was broken up, when he was invested by the organic law of the land with the title, dignity and immunity of an American citizen, and when it was declared that any discrimination made by any State against him on account of race or color was unlawful, I hold that his race condition could no longer be considered a problem. The thing was done: it was finished. The nation had taken its position and all the parts of the nation must ultimately adjust themselves to the whole. The individual States may be great, but the United States is greater. The mountain will not and cannot go to Mahomet, so Mahomet must and will in the end go to the mountain. Herein is the ground of my hope.

The trend of civilization, the power of large bodies to attract small ones, the force of national greatness, the inclination to the stronger rather than to the weak in human forces will ultimately bring the individual States in line with the Federal body. I affirm that while the National Government shall remain in the hands of the Republican party and under the principles of that party, no State will or can permanently disenfranchise any of its citizens because of race or color or previous condition. Attempts may be made to do this, but the race problem in that respect is solved, and the case cannot be permanently reopened.

But I am asked, what of the future? and will the various peoples of this country ever be thoroughly assimilated? or, to speak more plainly, will they ever intermarry? My answer is, "Sufficient unto the day is the evil thereof." We should not cross the stream till we have come to it. Whether such marriages will ever become common or not is no matter of vital concern to anybody at this day. It is mere speculation and is utterly without practical importance, so far as the rights of the American people are concerned. It touches no question of politics, statesmanship, or religion.

Individual interests, personal preferences and public sentiment may be safely left to regulate the relations of the races in respect of intermarriage. Such, I think, is the view that common sense will take of it, but such does not seem to be the view taken of it by some of our people—white, black and mixed. There seems to be a fascination about the subject which makes it impossible for men to let alone. They thrust it into our faces on all occasions, in season and out of season, and seem distressed because we cannot solve the problem for them. Some of them say that the repugnance of the white race of the black makes marriages between them impossible, and yet they proceed with great warmth and eloquence to denounce it as a thing to be closely watched and guarded against, and by no means encouraged. If the thing is impossible to happen no one should be afraid that it will happen.

I noticed while at my post in Haiti that even the Senate of the United States was compelled to listen to a learned disquisition upon this subject of race intermarriage from the lips of the eloquent, learned, and distinguished Senator from Kansas. I have always entertained for that gifted gentleman the highest respect. When he is right he is very right and when he is wrong he is very wrong. There is no halfness is his character and composition. He is either all or he is nothing. In the present instance he happens to be not only all wrong, but very wrong. His argument against the admixture of the race is intense but narrow, brilliant but unsound, learned but inconsistent and illogical. He not only contradicts the facts and the science of the case but contradicts himself. He asserts that only the bad qualities of each race are inherited by a mixed race, and at the same time he permits himself to say that he attributes whatever ability I happen to possess to the Caucasian side of my parentage. So good a logician as Senator Ingalls should not have allowed himself, almost in the same breath, to knock down the whole superstructure of his argument. Mr. Ingalls is a brave and a generous man, and I am surprised that these qualities were allowed to forsake him on the occasion referred to. Had he listened to the manly side of his character he would have never allowed himself to slay with his brilliant rhetoric a million of his colored fellow-citizens. He took advantage of his position on the floor of the United States Senate to deal us a blow which we had no means of parrying. His advantage was great, and the ignoble character of his attack must be measured by the greatness of his advantage. Had any colored man of spirit and ability been a member of the Senate to reply to his assault. Mr. Ingalls would not have been inconsistent with his well-known chivalric qualities. But the case was otherwise.

If it be true that good qualities are not transmissible in such unions; if it be true that only evil, and that continually, must descend to the children of such parents, it may be well asked why any of the mulatto or quadroon children and grandchildren of our earlier statesmen are found anywhere outside of the thick walls and iron-barred windows of our prisons. Why are they walking our streets and employed in our houses as trusted servants and stewards? Why are they our teachers, professors, and preachers? Why are they respected and treated as gentlemen and Christians in every part of the world except our own? Oh, no, Mr. Ingalls! Your argument will not hold. It will not bear the test of either reason or experience.

Your language is the language of alarm, and the question you should put to yourself is, What if, in a nation of a hundred millions there should occasionally happen a marriage between two different varieties of the human family? Who would be hurt by it? Who, outside the parties themselves, should give themselves any trouble about it? The sun would not cease to shine, the rain to descend, nor the grass to grow. Men would not cease to go to and fro in the earth, or knowledge cease to roll onward. If the country has endured, during 240 years, lawless relations on a broad scale between the two peoples, it should not go into paroxysms of alarm over what may possibly take place under lawful conditions.

And now comes Mr. Isaiah Montgomery, of Mississippi, with his solution of the pretended Negro problem. I have spoken of him elsewhere, and I take back nothing that I have said either of this remarkable man, or his remarkable address. He has surrendered to a disloyal State a great franchise given to himself and his people by the loyal nation. He has taken the work of solving the nation's work out of the nation's hands. He has virtually said to the nation: "You have done wrong in giving us this great liberty. You should give us back a part of our bondage." He has surrendered a part of his rights to an enemy who will make this surrender a reason for demanding all of his rights. He has conducted his people to a depth from which they will be invited to a lower deep, for if he can rightfully surrender a part of his heritage from the National Government at the bidding of his oppressors, he may surrender the whole. The people with whom he makes this deal are restrained in dealing with the rights of colored men by no sense of modesty or moderation in their demands. They want all that is to be had, and will take all that they can get. Their real sentiment is that no Negro shall or ought to have the right to vote. Yet I have no denunciation for the man Montgomery. He is not a conscious traitor though his act is treason: treason to the cause of the colored people, not only of his own State, but of the United States.

I wish the consequences of his act could be confined to Mississippi alone, but I fear this cannot be. Other colored men in other States, dazzled by the fame obtained by Mr. Montgomery through the Democratic press, will probably imitate his bad example. I speak of this Montgomery business more in sorrow than in anger. I hear in the plaintive eloquence of his marvelous address a groan of bitter anguish born of oppression and despair. It is the voice of a soul from which all hope has vanished. His deed kindles indignation to be sure, but his condition awakens pity. He had called to the nation for help—help which it ought to have rendered and could have rendered but it did not—and in a moment of impatience and despair he has thought to make terms with the enemy, an enemy with whom no colored man can make terms but by a sacrifice of his manhood. There is no need here of an analysis of Mr. Montgomery's address. Its character is known and it has nothing to commend it but its ability and plaintive eloquence and the man, the place, and the circumstances under which it was delivered. The logic of the speech would have conducted magnanimous men to a prompt rejection of the surrender, for it was an appeal to all that was noble, grateful, and generous in hearts of Mississippians. They should have said, "No, Mr. Montgomery; your people have been our best friends when we needed friends, and we scorn to take from you the franchise accorded to you by the wisdom and magnanimity of the National Government."

Ladies and gentlemen: I have been requested to say an encouraging word to our people before I leave for my post of duty at Port-au-Prince, and if I have not already said such a word I find it quite easy to do so now. From every view I have been able to take of the moral and political situation of our cause, before and since my arrival in the country, I am hopeful. I have no doubt whatever of the future. I know that there are times in the history of all reforms when the future looks dark; when

the friends of reform are impatient and despondent; when they
cannot see the end from the beginning; when the truth that is
plain to them compels them to reject the honesty of all
who receive it. When they meet with opposition where they
expected cooperation; when they met with treachery where
they expected fidelity, and defeat where they expected victory.
I, for one, have gone through all this. I have had fifty years of
it, and yet I have not lost either heart or hope. It is true that we
have been sadly disappointed in the action, or rather non-action,
of the Fifty-first Congress. The platform of the Republican party
adopted at Chicago plainly committed the Republican party to
some measure of protection to the Republican voters of the
South. We had right to expect the pledge there given would
find fulfillment in the action of this Republican Congress. We
have been disappointed, sadly disappointed. Following the
advice of a new leader from Pennsylvania, but a leader not of
the Thaddeus Stevens and Charles Sumner mold, this Congress
has preferred protection to commerce and property to protection
to personal and political liberty. We had hoped that it would
adopt either the Federal election bill or the Blair educational
bill. It has done neither. The omission is, on the face of it,
discouraging. But what then? Shall we get mad and denounce
and renounce the Republican party? Has that party sinned away
its day of grace? Are there no remaining reasons for giving it
our confidence? I entertain no such thought. The Federal election and educational bills are not dead, nor are their friends
idle. Mr. Cabot Lodge and Mr. Blair and their friends in the
Senate and in the House may permit delay but they will not
suffer defeat. The president of the United States is true to his
trust. No man since General Grant has stood by us more firmly
than has General Harrison. He has let it be known openly and
emphatically that he is for stepping to the very verge of constitutional limitations to secure honest elections, a free vote,
and a fair count in every State in the Union, and he is not the
man to take any steps backward.

I admit that during many years to come the colored man will have to endure prejudice against his race and color, but this constitutes no problem to vex and disturb the course of legislation. The world was never yet without prejudice. There exists prejudice in favor of and against classes among men of the same race and color. There is prejudice between religious sects and denominations; between Catholic and Protestant; between families and individuals. The time may never come this side the millennium when men will not ask "Can any good thing come out of Nazareth?" But what business has government, State or National, with these prejudices? Why should grave statesmen concern themselves with them? The business of government is to hold its broad shield over all and to see that every American citizen is alike and equally protected in his civil and personal rights. My confidence is strong and high in the nation as a whole. I believe in its justice and in its power. I believe that it means to keep its word with its colored citizens. I believe in its progress, in its moral as well as its material civilization. Its trend is in the right direction. Its fundamental principles are sound. Its conception of humanity and of human rights is clear and comprehensive. Its progress is fettered by no State religion tending to repress liberal thought: by no order of nobility tending to keep down the toiling masses: by no divine right theory tending to national stagnation under the idea of stability. It stands out free and clear with nothing to obstruct its view of the lessons of reason and experience.

It may be said, as has been said, that I am growing old, and am easily satisfied with things as they are. When our young men shall have worked and waited for victory as long as I have worked and waited, they will not only learn to have patience with the men opposed to them, but with me also for having patience with such. I have seen dark hours in my life, and I have seen the darkness gradually disappearing and the light gradually increasing. One by one I have seen obstacles removed, errors corrected, prejudices softened, proscriptions relinquished, and my people advancing in all the elements that go to make up the sum of general welfare. And I remember that God reigns in eternity, and that whatever delays, whatever disappointments and discouragements may come, truth, justice, liberty and humanity will ultimately prevail.

Self-Made Men
(1894)

In this motivational masterpiece, Frederick Douglass provides an inspirational account of his own rise from slavery to success, while providing an explanation of how the key to overcoming even the lowest of origins is, in his words, "Work! Work!! Work!!! Work!!!!" While Douglass spoke on this subject many times throughout his life, the following address was delivered on April 6, 1894, just 10 months before his death, at the Indian Industrial School in Carlisle, Pennsylvania.

THE SUBJECT ANNOUNCED for this evening's entertainment is not new. Man in one form or another, has been a frequent and fruitful subject for the press, the pulpit and the platform. This subject has come up for consideration under a variety of attractive titles, such as "Great Men," "Representative Men," "Peculiar Men," "Scientific Men," "Literary Men," "Successful Men," "Men of Genius," and "Men of the World;" but under whatever name or designation, the vital point of interest in the discussion has ever been the same, and that is, manhood itself, and this in its broadest and most comprehensive sense.

This tendency to the universal, in such discussion, is altogether natural and all controlling; for when we consider what man, as a whole, is; what he has been; what he aspires to be, and what, by a wise and vigorous cultivation of his faculties, he may yet become, we see that it leads irresistibly to this broad view of him as a subject of thought and inquiry.

The saying of the poet that "The proper study of mankind is man," and which has been the starting point of so many lectures, essays and speeches, holds its place, like all other great utterances, because it contains a great truth and a truth alike for every age and generation of men. It is always new and can never grow old. It is neither dimmed by time nor tarnished by repetition; for man, both in respect of himself and of his species, is now, and evermore will be, the center of unsatisfied human curiosity.

The pleasure we derive from any department of knowledge is largely due to the glimpse which it gives to us of our own nature. We may travel far over land and sea, brave all climates, dare all dangers, endure all hardships, try all latitudes and longitudes; we may penetrate the earth, sound the ocean's depths and sweep the hollow sky with our glasses, in the pursuit of other knowledge; we may contemplate the glorious landscape gemmed by forest, lake and river and dotted with peaceful homes and quiet herds; we may whirl away to the great cities, all aglow with life and enterprise; we may mingle with the imposing assemblages of wealth and power; we may visit the halls where Art works her miracles in music, speech and color, and where Science unbars the gates to higher planes of civilization; but no matter how radiant the colors, how enchanting the melody, how gorgeous and splendid the pageant; man himself, with eyes turned inward upon his own wondrous attributes and powers surpasses them all. A single human soul standing here upon the margin we call TIME, overlooking, in the vastness of its range, the solemn past which can neither be recalled nor remodelled, ever chafing against finite limitations, entangled with interminable contradictions, eagerly seeking to scan the invisible past and to pierce the clouds and darkness of the ever mysterious future, has attractions for thought and study, more numerous and powerful than all other objects beneath the sky. To human thought and inquiry he is broader than all visible worlds, loftier than all heights and deeper than all depths. Were I called upon to point out the broadest and most permanent distinction between mankind and other animals, it would be this; their earnest desire for the fullest knowledge of human nature on all its many sides. The importance of this knowledge is immeasurable, and by no other is human life so affected and colored. Nothing can bring to man so much of happiness or so much of misery as man himself. Today he exalts himself to heaven by his virtues and achievements; tomorrow he smiles with sadness and pain, by his crimes and follies. But whether exalted or debased, charitable or wicked; whether saint or villain, priest or prize fighter; if only he be great in his line, he is an unfailing source of interest, as one of a common brotherhood; for the best man finds in his breast the evidence of kinship with the worst, and the worst with the best. Confront us with either extreme and you will rivet our attention and fix us in earnest contemplation, for our chief desire is to know what there is in man and to know him at all extremes and ends and opposites, and for this knowledge, or for the want of it, we will follow him from the gates of life to the gates of death, and beyond them.

As this subject can never become old, so it can never be exhausted. Man is too closely related to the Infinite to be divided, weighed, measured and reduced to fixed standards, and thus adjusted to finite comprehension. No two of anything are exactly alike, and what is true of man in one generation may lack some degree of truth in another, but his distinctive qualities as man, are inherent and remain forever. Progressive in his nature, he defies the power of progress to overtake him to make known, definitely, the limits of his marvellous powers and possibilities.

From man comes all that we know or can imagine of heaven and earth, of time and eternity. He is the prolific constituter of manners, morals, religions and governments. He spins them out as the spider spins his web, and they are coarse or fine, kind or cruel, according to the degree of intelligence reached by him at the period of their establishment. He compels us to contemplate his past with wonder and to survey his future with much the same feelings as those with which Columbus is supposed to have gazed westward over the sea. It is the faith of the race that in man there exists far outlying continents of power, thought and feeling, which remain to be discovered, explored, cultivated, made practical and glorified.

Mr. Emerson has declared that it is natural to believe in great men. Whether this is a fact, or not, we do believe in them and worship them. The Visible God of the New Testament is revealed to us as a man of like passions with ourselves. We seek out our wisest and best man, the man who, by eloquence or the sword compels us to believe him such, and make him our leader, prophet, preacher and law giver. We do this, not because he is essentially different from us, but because of his identity with us. He is our best representative and reflects, on a colossal scale, the scale to which we would aspire, our highest aims, objects, powers and possibilities.

This natural reverence for all that is great in man, and this tendency to deify and worship him, though natural and the source of man's elevation, has not always shown itself wise but has often shown itself far otherwise than wise. It has often given us a wicked ruler for a righteous one, a false prophet for a true one, a corrupt preacher for a pure one, a man of war for a man of peace, and a distorted and vengeful image of God for an image of justice and mercy.

But it is not my purpose to attempt here any comprehensive and exhaustive theory or philosophy of the nature of manhood in all the range I have indicated. I am here to speak to you of a peculiar type of manhood under the title of

SELF-MADE MEN

That there is, in more respects than one, something like a solecism in this title, I freely admit. Properly speaking, there are in the world no such men as self-made men. That term implies an individual independence of the past and present which can never exist.

Our best and most valued acquisitions have been obtained either from our contemporaries or from those who have preceded us in the field of thought and discovery. We have all either begged, borrowed or stolen. We have reaped where others have sown, and that which others have strown, we have gathered. It must in truth be said though it may not accord well with self-conscious individuality and self-conceit, that no possible native force of character, and no depth or wealth of originality, can lift a man into absolute independence of his fellow men, and no generation of men can be independent of the preceding generation. The brotherhood and inter-dependence of mankind are guarded and defended at all points. I believe in individuality, but individuals are, to the mass, like waves to the ocean. The highest order of genius is as dependent as is the lowest. It, like the loftiest waves of the sea, derives its power and greatness from the grandeur and vastness of the ocean of which it forms a part. We differ as the waves, but are one as the sea. To do something well does not necessarily imply the ability to do everything else equally well. If you can do in one direction that which I cannot do, I may in another direction, be able to do that which you cannot do. Thus the balance of power is kept comparatively even, and a self-acting brotherhood and inter-dependence is maintained.

Nevertheless, the title of my lecture is eminently descriptive of a class and is, moreover, a fit and convenient one for my purpose, in illustrating the idea which I have in view. In the order of discussion I shall adopt the style of an old-fashioned preacher and have a "firstly," a "secondly," a "thirdly," a "fourthly" and, possibly, a "conclusion."

My first is, "Who are self-made men?" My second is, "What is the true theory of their success?" My third is, "The advantages which self-made men derive from the manners and institutions of their surroundings," and my fourth is, "The grounds of the criticism to which they are, as a class, especially exposed."

On the first point I may say that, by the term "self-made men," I mean especially what, to the popular mind, the term itself imports. Self-made men are the men who, under peculiar difficulties and without the ordinary helps of favoring circumstances, have attained knowledge, usefulness, power and position and have learned from themselves the best uses to which life can be put in this world, and in the exercises of these uses to build up worthy character. They are the men who owe little or nothing to birth, relationship, friendly surroundings; to wealth inherited or to early approved means of education; who are what they are, without the aid of any of the favoring conditions by which other men usually rise in the world and achieve great results. In fact they are the men who are not brought up but who are obliged to come up, not only without the voluntary assistance or friendly cooperation of society, but often in open and derisive defiance of all the efforts of society and the tendency of circumstances to repress, retard and keep them down. They are the men who, in a world of schools, academies, colleges and other institutions of learning, are often compelled by unfriendly circumstances to acquire their education elsewhere and, amidst unfavorable conditions, to hew out for themselves a way to success, and thus to become the architects of their own good fortunes. They are in a peculiar sense, indebted to themselves for themselves. If they have traveled far, they have made the road on which they traveled. If they have ascended high, they have built their own ladder. From the depths of poverty such as these have often come. From the heartless pavements of large and crowded cities; barefooted, homeless, and friendless, they have come. From hunger, rags and destitution, they have come; motherless and fatherless, they have come, and may come. Flung overboard in the midnight storm on the broad and tempest-tossed ocean of life; left without ropes, planks, oars or life-preservers, they have bravely buffetted the frowning billows and have risen in safety and life where others, supplied with the best appliances for safety and success, have fainted, despaired and gone down forever.

Such men as these, whether found in one position or another, whether in the college or in the factory; whether professors or plowmen; whether Caucasian or Indian; whether Anglo-Saxon or Anglo-African, are self-made men and are entitled to a certain measure of respect for their success and for proving to the world the grandest possibilities of human nature, of whatever variety of race or color.

Though a man of this class need not claim to be a hero or to be worshiped as such, there is genuine heroism in his struggle and something of sublimity and glory in his triumph. Every instance of such success is an example and a help to humanity. It, better than any mere assertion, gives us assurance of the latent powers and resources of simple and unaided manhood. It dignifies labor, honors application, lessens pain and depression, dispels gloom from the brow of the destitute and weariness from the heart of him about to faint, and enables man to take hold of the roughest and flintiest hardships incident to the battle of life, with a lighter heart, with higher hopes and a larger courage.

But I come at once to the second part of my subject, which respects the

THEORY OF SELF-MADE MEN

"Upon what meat doth this, our CÆSAR, feed, he hath grown so great?" How happens it that the cottager is often found equal to the lord, and that, in the race of life, the sons of the poor often get even with, and surpass even, the sons of the rich? How happens it from the field often come statesmen equal to those from the college? I am sorry to say that, upon this interesting point, I can promise nothing absolute nor anything which will be entirely satisfactory and conclusive. Burns says:

> "I see how folks live that hae riches,
> But surely poor folks maun be witches."

The various conditions of men and the different uses they make of their powers and opportunities in life, are full of puzzling contrasts and contradictions. Here, as elsewhere, it is easy to dogmatize, but it is not so easy to define, explain and demonstrate. The natural laws for the government, well-being and progress of mankind, seem to be equal and are equal; but the subjects of these laws everywhere abound in inequalities, discords and contrasts. We cannot have fruit without flowers, but we often have flowers without fruit. The promise of youth often breaks down in manhood, and real excellence often comes unheralded and from unexpected quarters.

The scene presented from this view is as a thousand arrows shot from the same point and aimed at the same object. United in aim, they are divided in flight. Some fly too high, others too low. Some go to the right, others to the left. Some fly too far and others, not far enough, and only a few hit the mark. Such is life. United in the quiver, they are divided in the air. Matched when dormant, they are unmatched in action.

When we attempt to account for greatness we never get nearer to the truth than did the greatest of poets and philosophers when he classified the conditions of greatness: "Some are born great, some achieve greatness and some have greatness thrust upon them." We may take our choice of these three separate explanations and make which of them we please, most prominent in our discussion. Much can certainly be said of superior mental endowments, and I should on some accounts, lean strongly to that theory, but for numerous examples which seem to, and do, contradict it, and but for the depressing tendency such a theory must have upon humanity generally.

This theory has truth in it, but it is not the whole truth. Men of very ordinary faculties have, nevertheless, made a very respectable way in the world and have sometimes presented even brilliant examples of success. On the other hand, what is called genius is often found by the wayside, a miserable wreck; the more deplorable and shocking because from the height from which it has fallen and the loss and ruin involved in the fall. There is, perhaps, a compensation in disappointment and in the contradiction of means to ends and promise to performance. These imply a constant effort on the part of nature to hold the balance evenly between all her children and to bring success within the reach of the humblest as well as of the most exalted.

From apparently the basest metals we have the finest toned bells, and we are taught respect from simple manhood when we see how, from the various dregs of society, there come men who may well be regarded as the pride and as the watch towers of the race.

Steel is improved by laying on damp ground, and the rusty razor gets a keener edge after giving its dross to the dirt in which it has been allowed to lie neglected and forgotten. In like manner, too, humanity, though it lay among the pots, covered with the dust of neglect and poverty, may still retain the divine impulse and the element of improvement and progress. It is natural to revolt at squalor, but we may well relax our lip of scorn and contempt when we stand among the lowly and despised, for out of the rags of the meanest cradle there may come a great man and this is a treasure richer than all the wealth of the Orient.

I do not think much of the accident or good luck theory of self-made men. It is worth but little attention and has no practical value. An apple carelessly flung into a crowd may hit one person, or it may hit another, or it may hit nobody. The probabilities are precisely the same in this accident theory of self-made men. It divorces a man from his own achievements, contemplates him as a being of chance and leaves him without will, motive, ambition and aspiration. Yet the accident theory is among the most popular theories of individual success. It has about it the air of mystery which the multitude so well like, and withal, it does something to mar the complacency of the successful.

It is one of the easiest and commonest things in the world for a successful man to be followed in his career through life and to have constantly pointed out this or that particular stroke of good fortune which fixed his destiny and made him successful. If not ourselves great, we like to explain why others are so. We are stingy in our praise to merit, but generous in our praise to chance. Besides, a man feels himself measurably great when he can point out the precise moment and circumstance which made his neighbor great. He easily fancies that the slight difference between himself and his friend is simply one of luck. It was his friend who was lucky but it might easily have been himself. Then too, the next best thing to success is a valid apology for non-success. Detraction is, to many, a delicious morsel. The excellence which it loudly denies to others it silently claims for itself. It possesses the means of covering the small with the glory of the great. It adds to failure that which it takes from success and shortens the distance between those in front and those in the rear. Even here there is an upward tendency worthy of notice and respect. The kitchen is ever the critic of the parlor. The talk of those below is of those above. We imitate those we revere and admire.

But the main objection to this very comfortable theory is that, like most other theories, it is made to explain too much. While it ascribes success to chance and friendly circumstances, it is apt to take no cognizance of the very different uses to which different men put their circumstances and their chances.

Fortune may crowd a man's life with favorable circumstances and happy opportunities, but they will, as all know, avail him nothing unless he makes a wise and vigorous use of them. It does not matter that the wind is fair and the tide at its flood, if the mariner refuses to weigh his anchor and spread his canvas to the breeze. The golden harvest is ripe in vain if the farmer refuses to reap. Opportunity is important but exertion is indispensable. "There is a tide in the affairs of men which, taken at its flood, leads on to fortune;" but it must be taken at its flood.

Within this realm of man's being, as elsewhere, Science is diffusing its broad, beneficent light. As this light increases, dependence upon chance or luck is destined to vanish and the wisdom of adapting means to ends, to become more manifest.

It was once more common than it is now, to hear men religiously ascribing their good or ill fortune directly to supernatural intervention. Success and failure, wealth and poverty, intelligence and ignorance, liberty and slavery, happiness and misery, were all bestowed or inflicted upon individual men by a divine hand and for all-wise purposes. Man was, by such reasoners, made a very insignificant agent in his own affairs. It was all the Lord's doings and marvellous to human eyes. Of course along with this superstition came the fortune teller, the pretender to divination and the miracle working priest who could save from famine by praying easier than by under-draining and deep plowing.

In such matter a wise man has little use for altars or oracle. He knows that the laws of God are perfect and unchangeable. He knows that health is maintained by right living; that disease is cured by the right use of remedies; that bread is produced by tilling the soil; that knowledge is obtained by study; that wealth is secured by saving and that battles are won by fighting. To him, the lazy man is the unlucky man and the man of luck is the man of work.

> "The fault, dear Brutus, is not in our stars,
> But in ourselves, that we are underlings."

When we find a man who has ascended heights beyond ourselves; who has a broader range of vision than we and a sky with more stars in it than we have in ours, we may know that he has worked harder, better and more wisely than we. He was awake while we slept. He was busy while we were idle and he was wisely improving his time and talents while we were wasting ours. Paul Dunbar, the colored poet, has well said:

> "There are no beaten paths to glory's height,
> There are no rules to compass greatness known;
> Each for himself must cleave a path alone,
> And press his own way forward in the fight.

> Smooth is the way to ease and calm delight,
> And soft the road Sloth chooseth for her own;
> But he who craves the flow'r of life full-blown
> Must struggle up in all his armor dight.
> What tho' the burden bear him sorely down,
> And crush to dust the mountain of his pride.
> Oh! then with strong heart let him still abide
> For rugged is the road way to renown.
> Nor may he hope to gain the envied crown
> Till he hath thrust the looming rocks aside."

I am certain that there is nothing good, great or desirable which man can possess in this world, that does not come by some kind of labor, either physical or mental, moral or spiritual. A man may, at times, get something for nothing, but it will, in his hands, amount to nothing. What is true in the world of matter, is equally true in the world of mind. Without culture there can be no growth; without exertion, no acquisition; without friction, no polish; without labor, no knowledge; without action, no progress and without conflict, no victory. The man who lies down a fool at night, hoping that he will waken wise in the morning, will rise up in the morning as he laid down in the evening.

Faith, in the absence of work, seems to be worth little, if anything. The preacher who finds it easier to pray for knowledge than to tax his brain with study and application will find his congregation growing beautifully less and his flock looking elsewhere for their spiritual and mental food. In the old slave times colored ministers were somewhat remarkable for the fervor with which they prayed for knowledge, but it did not appear that they were remarkable for any wonderful success. In fact, they who prayed loudest seemed to get least. They thought if they opened their mouths they would be filled. The result was an abundance of sound with a great destitution of sense.

Not only in man's experience, but also in nature do we find exemplified the truth upon which I have been insisting. My father worketh, said the Savior, and I also work. In every view which we obtain of the perfections of the universe; whether we look to the bright stars in the peaceful blue dome above us, or to the long shore line of the ocean, where land and water maintain eternal conflict; the lesson taught is the same; that of endless action and reaction. Those beautifully rounded pebbles which you gather on the sand and which you hold in your hand and marvel at their exceeding smoothness, were chiseled into their varied and graceful forms by the ceaseless action of countless waves. Nature is herself a great worker and never tolerates, without certain rebuke, any contradiction to her wise example. Inaction is followed by stagnation. Stagnation is followed by pestilence and pestilence is followed by death. General Butler, busy with his broom, could sweep yellow fever out of New Orleans, but this dread destroyer returned when the General and his broom were withdrawn, and the people, neglecting sanitary wisdom, went on ascribing to Divinity what was simply due to dirt.

From these remarks it will be evident that, allowing only ordinary ability and opportunity, we may explain success mainly by one word and that word is WORK! WORK!! WORK!!! WORK!!!! Not transient and fitful effort, but patient, enduring, honest, unremitting and indefatigable work, into which the whole heart is put, and which, in both temporal and spiritual affairs, is the true miracle worker. Every one may avail himself of this marvellous power, if he will. There is no royal road to perfection. Certainly no one must wait for some kind friend to put a springing board under his feet, upon which he may easily bound from the first round of the ladder onward and upward to its highest round. If he waits for this, he may wait long and perhaps forever. He who does not think himself worth saving from poverty and ignorance, by his own efforts, will hardly be thought worth the efforts of anybody else.

The lesson taught at this point by human experience is simply this, that the man who will get up will be helped up; and that the man who will not get up will be allowed to stay down. This rule may appear somewhat harsh, but in its general application and operation it is wise, just and beneficent. I know of no other rule which can be substituted for it without bringing social chaos. Personal independence is a virtue and it is the soul out of which comes the sturdiest manhood. But there can be no independence without a large share of self-dependence, and this virtue cannot be bestowed. It must be developed from within.

I have been asked "How will this theory affect the Negro?" and "What shall be done in his case?" My general answer is "Give the Negro fair play and let him alone. If he lives, well. If he dies, equally well. If he cannot stand up, let him fall down."

The apple must have strength and vitality enough in itself to hold on, or it will fall to the ground where it belongs. The strongest influence prevails and should prevail. If the vital relation of the fruit is severed, it is folly to tie the stem to the branch or the branch to the tree or to shelter the fruit from the wind. So, too, there is no wisdom in lifting from the earth a head which must only fall the more heavily when the help is withdrawn. Do right, though the heavens fall; but they will not fall.

I have said "Give the Negro fair play and let him alone." I meant all that I said and a good deal more than some understand by fair play. It is not fair play to start the Negro out in life, from nothing and with nothing, while others start with the advantage of a thousand years behind them. He should be measured, not by the heights others have obtained, but from the depths from which he has come. For any adjustment of the seals of comparison, fair play demands that to the barbarism from which the Negro started shall be added two hundred years heavy with human bondage. Should the American people put a school house in every valley of the South and a church on every hill side and supply the one with teachers and the other with preachers, for a hundred years to come, they would not then have given fair play to the Negro.

The nearest approach to justice to the Negro for the past is to do him justice in the present. Throw open to him the doors of the schools, the factories, the workshops, and of all mechanical industries. For his own welfare, give him a chance to do whatever he can do well. If he fails then, let him fail! I can, however, assure you that he will not fail. Already has he proven it. As a soldier he proved it. He has since proved it by industry and sobriety and by the acquisition of knowledge and property. He is almost the only successful tiller of the soil of the South, and is fast becoming the owner of land formerly owned by his old master and by the old master class. In a thousand instances has he verified my theory of self-made men. He well performed the task of making bricks without straw: now give him straw. Give him all the facilities for honest and successful livelihood, and in all honorable avocations receive him as a man among men.

I have by implication admitted that work alone is not the only explanation of self-made men, or of the secret of success. Industry, to be sure, is the superficial and visible cause of success, put what is the cause of industry? In the answer to this question one element is easily pointed out, and that element is necessity. Thackeray very wisely remarks that "All men are about as lazy as they can afford to be." Men cannot be depended upon to work when they are asked to work for nothing. They are not only as lazy as they can afford to be, but I have found many who were a great deal more so. We all hate the task master, but all men, however industrious, are either lured or lashed through the world, and we should be a lazy, good-for-nothing set, if we were not so lured and lashed.

Necessity is not only the mother of invention, but the mainspring of exertion. The presence of some urgent, pinching, imperious necessity, will often not only sting a man into marvellous exertion, but into a sense of the possession, within himself, of powers and resources which else had slumbered on through a long life, unknown to himself and never suspected by others. A man never knows the strength of his grip till life and limb depend upon it. Something is likely to be done when something must be done.

If you wish to make your son helpless, you need not cripple him with bullet or bludgeon, but simply place him beyond the reach of necessity and surround him with ease and luxury. This experiment has often been tried and has seldom failed. As a general rule, where circumstances do most for men, there man will do least for himself; and where man does least, he himself is least. His doing or not doing makes or unmakes him.

Under the palm trees of Africa man finds, without effort, food, raiment and shelter. For him, there, Nature has done all and he has done nothing. The result is that the glory of Africa is in her palms,—and not in her men.

In your search after manhood go not to those delightful latitudes where "summer is blossoming all the year long," but rather to the hardy North, to Maine, New Hampshire and Vermont, to the coldest and flintiest parts of New England, where men work gardens with gunpowder, blast rocks to find places to plant potatoes; where, for six months of the year, the earth is covered with snow and ice. Go to the states which Daniel Webster thought good enough to emigrate from, and there you will find the highest type of American physical and intellectual manhood.

Happily for mankind, labor not only supplies the good things for which it is exerted, but it increases its own resources and improves, sharpens and strengthens its own instruments.

The primary condition upon which men have and retain power and skill is exertion. Nature has no use for unused power. She abhors a vacuum. She permits no preemption without occupation. Every organ of body and mind has its use and improves by use. "Better to wear out than to rust out," is sound philosophy as well as common sense. The eye of the watch-maker is severely taxed by the intense light and effort necessary in order to see minute objects, yet it remains clear and keen long after those of other men have failed. I was told at the Remington Rifle Works, by the workmen there employed who have to straighten the rifle barrels by flashing intense light through them, that, by this practice, severe as it seems, their eyes were made stronger.

But what the hands find to do must be done in earnest. Nature tolerates no halfness. He who wants hard hands must not, at sight of the first blister, fling away the spade, the rake, the broad axe or the hoe; for the blister is a primary condition to the needed hardness. To abandon work is not only to throw away the means of success, but it is also to part with the ability to work. To be able to walk well, one must walk on, and to work with ease and effect, one must work on.

Thus the law of labor is self-acting, beneficent and perfect; increasing skill and ability according to exertion. Faithful, earnest and protracted industry gives strength to the mind and facility to the hand. Within certain limits, the more that a man does, the more he can do.

Few men ever reach, in any one direction, the limits of their possibilities. As in commerce, so here, the relation of supply to demand rules. Our mechanical and intellectual forces increase or decrease according to the demands made upon them. He who uses most will have most to use. This is the philosophy of the parable of the ten talents. It applies here as elsewhere. "To him that hath shall be given and from him that hath not shall be taken even that which he hath."

Exertion of muscle or mind, for pleasure and amusement alone, cannot bring anything like the good results of earnest labor. Such exertion lacks the element attached to duty. To play perfectly upon any complicated instrument, one must play long, laboriously and with earnest purpose. Though it be an amusement at first, it must be labor at the end, if any proficiency is reached. If one plays for one's own pleasure alone, the performance will give little pleasure to any one else and will finally become a rather hard and dry pleasure to one's self.

In this respect one cannot receive much more than one gives. Men may cheat their neighbors and may cheat themselves but they cannot cheat nature. She will only pay the wages one honestly earns.

In the idea of exertion, of course fortitude and perseverance are included. We have all met a class of men, very remarkable for their activity, and who yet make but little headway in life; men who, in their noisy and impulsive pursuit of knowledge, never get beyond the outer bark of an idea, from a lack of patience and perseverance to dig to the core; men who begin everything and complete nothing; who see, but do not perceive; who read, but forget what they read, and are as if they had not read; who travel, but go nowhere in particular, and have nothing of value to impart when they return. Such men may have greatness thrust upon them but they never achieve greatness.

As the gold in the mountain is concealed in huge and flinty rocks, so the most valuable ideas and inventions are often enveloped in doubt and uncertainty. The printing press, the sewing machine, the railroad, the telegraph and the locomotive, are all simple enough now, but who can measure the patience, the persistence, the fortitude, the wearing labor and the brain sweat, which produced these wonderful and indispensable additions to our modern civilization.

My theory of self-made men is, then, simply this; that they are men of work. Whether or not such men have acquired material, moral or intellectual excellence, honest labor faithfully, steadily and persistently pursued, is the best, if not the only, explanation of their success. But in thus awarding praise to industry, as the main agency in the production and culture of self-made men, I do not exclude other factors of the problem. I only make them subordinate. Other agencies cooperate, but this is the principal one and the one without which all others would fail.

Indolence and failure can give a thousand excuses for themselves. How often do we hear men say, "If I had the head of this

one, or the hands of that one; the health of this one, or the
strength of that one; the chances of this or of that one, I might
have been this, that, or the other;" and much more of the same
sort.

Sound bodily health and mental faculties unimpaired are very
desirable, if not absolutely indispensable. But a man need not
be a physical giant or an intellectual prodigy, in order to make
a tolerable way in the world. The health and strength of the
soul is of far more importance than is that of the body, even
when viewed as a means of mundane results. The soul is the
main thing. Man can do a great many things; some easily and
some with difficulty, but he cannot build a sound ship with
rotten timber. Her model may be faultless; her spars may be
the finest and her canvas the whitest and the flags of all nations
may be displayed at her masthead, but she will go down in the
first storm. So it is with the soul. Whatever its assumptions,
if it be lacking in the principles of honor, integrity and affection,
it, too, will go down in the first storm. And when the soul is
lost, all is lost. All human experience proves over and over again,
that any success which comes through meanness, trickery, fraud
and dishonor, is but emptiness and will only be a torment to
its possessor.

Let not the morally strong, though physically weak abandon
the struggle of life. For such happily, there is both place and
chance in the world. The highest services to man and the richest
rewards to the worker are not conditioned entirely upon physical
power. The higher the plane of civilization, the more abundant
the opportunities of the weak and infirm. Society and civilization
move according to celestial order. "Not that which is spiritual
is first, but that which is natural. After that, that which is
spiritual." The order of progress, is, first, barbarism; afterward,
civilization. Barbarism represents physical force. Civilization
represents spiritual power. The primary condition, that of barbarism, knows no other law than that of force; not right, but
might. In this condition of society, or rather of no society, the

man of mind is pushed aside by the man of muscle. A Kit Carson, far out on the borders of civilization, dexterously handling his bowie knife, rifle and bludgeon, easily gets himself taken for a hero; but the waves of science and civilization rolling out over the Western prairies, soon leave him no room for his barbarous accomplishment. Kit is shorn of his glory. A higher type of manhood is required.

Where ferocious beasts and savage inhabitants have been dispersed and the rudeness of nature has been subdued, we welcome milder methods and gentler instrumentalities for the service of mankind. Here the race is not to the swift nor the battle to the strong, but the prize is brought within the reach of those who are neither swift nor strong. None need despair. There is room and work for all: for the weak as well as the strong. Activity is the law for all and its rewards are open to all. Vast acquirements and splendid achievements stand to the credit of men of feeble frames and slender constitutions. Channing was physically weak. Milton was blind. Montgomery was small and effeminate. But these men were more to the world than a thousand Sampsons. Mrs. Stowe would be nothing among the grizzly bears of the Rocky mountains. We should not be likely to ask for her help at a barn raising, or a ship launch; but when a great national evil was to be removed; when a nation's heart was to be touched; when a whole country was to be redeemed and regenerated and millions of slaves converted into free men, the civilized world knew no earthly power equal to hers.

But another element of the secret of success demands a word. That element is order, systematic endeavor. We succeed, not alone by the laborious exertion of our faculties, be they small or great, but by the regular, thoughtful and systematic exercise of them. Order, the first law of heaven, is itself a power. The battle is nearly lost when your lines are in disorder. Regular, orderly and systematic effort which moves without friction and needless loss of time or power; which has a place for everything and everything in its place; which knows just where to begin, how to proceed and where to end, though marked by no extraordinary outlay of energy or activity, will work wonders, not only in the matter of accomplishment, but also in the increase of the ability of the individual. It will make the weak man strong and the strong man stronger; the simple man wise and the wise man, wiser, and will insure success by the power and influence that belong to habit.

On the other hand, no matter what gifts and what aptitudes a man may possess; no matter though his mind be of the highest order and fitted for the noblest achievements; yet, without this systematic effort, his genius will only serve as a fire of shavings, soon in blaze and soon out.

Spontaneity has a special charm, and the fitful outcroppings of genius are, in speech or action, delightful; but the success attained by these is neither solid nor lasting. A man who, for nearly forty years, was the foremost orator in New England, was asked by me, if his speeches were extemporaneous? They flowed so smoothly that I had my doubts about it. He answered, "No, I carefully think out and write my speeches, before I utter them." When such a man rises to speak, he knows what he is going to say. When he speaks, he knows what he is saying. When he retires from the platform, he knows what he *has* said.

There is still another element essential to success, and that is, a commanding object and a sense of its importance. The vigor of the action depends upon the power of the motive. The wheels of the locomotive lie idle upon the rail until they feel the impelling force of the steam; but when that is applied, the whole ponderous train is set in motion. But energy ought not to be wasted. A man may dispose of his life as Paddy did of his powder,—aim at nothing, and hit it every time.

If each man in the world did his share of honest work, we should have no need of a millennium. The world would teem with abundance, and the temptation to evil in a thousand directions, would disappear. But work is not often undertaken for its own sake. The worker is conscious of an object worthy of effort, and works for that object; not for what he is to it, but for what it is to him. All are not moved by the same objects. Happiness is the object of some. Wealth and fame are the objects of others. But wealth and fame are beyond the reach of the majority of men, and thus, to them, these are not motive-impelling objects. Happily, however, personal, family and neighborhood well-being stand near to us all and are full of lofty inspirations to earnest endeavor, if we would but respond to their influence.

I do not desire my lecture to become a sermon; but, were this allowable, I would rebuke the growing tendency to sport and pleasure. The time, money and strength devoted to these phantoms, would banish darkness and hunger from every hearthstone in our land. Multitudes, unconscious of any controlling object in life, flit, like birds, from point to point; now here, now there; and so accomplish nothing, either here or there.

> "For pleasures are like poppies spread,
> You seize the flower, its bloom is shed!
> Or like the snow-falls in the river,
> A moment white—then melts forever;
> Or like the borealis race,
> That flit ere you can point their place;
> Or like the rainbow's lovely form
> Evanishing amid the storm.—"

They know most of pleasure who seek it least, and they least who seek it most. The cushion is soft to him who sits on it but seldom. The men behind the chairs at Saratoga and Newport, get better dinners than the men in them. We cannot serve two masters. When here, we cannot be there. If we accept ease, we must part with appetite. A pound of feathers is as heavy as a pound of iron,—and about as hard, if you sit on it long enough. Music is delightful, but too much of it wounds the ear like the filing of a saw. The lounge, to the lazy, becomes like flint; and to him, the most savory dishes lose their flavor.

> "It's true, they need na starve or sweat,
> Thro' winter's cauld or simmer's heat;
> But human bodies are sic fools,
> For all their colleges an' schools,
> That when na real ills perplex them,
> They make now, themselves to vex them."

But the industrious man does find real pleasure. He finds it in qualities and quantities to which the baffled pleasure seeker is a perpetual stranger. He finds it in the house well built, in the farm well tilled, in the books well kept, in the page well written, in the thought well expressed, in all the improved conditions of life around him and in whatsoever useful work may, for the moment, engage his time and energies.

I will give you, in one simple statement, my idea, my observation and my experience of the chief agent in the success of self-made men. It is not luck, nor is it great mental endowments, but it is well directed, honest toil. "Toil and Trust!" was the motto of John Quincy Adams, and his Presidency of the Republic proved its wisdom as well as its truth. Great in his opportunities, great in his mental endowments and great in his relationships, he was still greater in persevering and indefatigable industry.

Examples of successful self-culture and self-help under great difficulties and discouragements, are abundant, and they vindicate the theory of success thus feebly and with homely common sense, presented. For example: Hugh Miller, whose lamented death mantled the mountains and valleys of his native land with a broad shadow of sorrow, scarcely yet lifted, was a grand example of the success of persistent devotion, under great difficulties, to work and to the acquisition of knowledge. In a country justly distinguished for its schools and colleges, he, like Robert Burns, Scotia's matchless son of song, was the true child of science, as Burns was of song. He was his own college. The earth was his school and the rocks were his school master. Outside of all the learned institutions of his country, and while employed with his chisel and hammer, as a stone mason, this man literally killed two birds with one stone; for he earned his daily bread and at the same time made himself an eminent geologist, and gave to the world books which are found in all public libraries and which are full of inspiration to the truth seeker.

Not unlike the case of Hugh Miller, is that of our own Elihu Burritt. The true heart warms with admiration for the energy and perseverance displayed in this man's pursuit of knowledge. We call him "The learned blacksmith," and the distinction was fairly earned and fitly worn. Over the polished anvil and glowing forge; amidst the smoke, dust and din of the blacksmith's shop; amidst its blazing fires and hissing sparks, and while hammering the red-hot steel, this brave son of toil is said to have mastered twenty different languages, living and dead.

It is surprising with what small means, in the field of earnest effort, great results have been achieved. That neither costly apparatus nor packed libraries are necessarily required by the earnest student in self-culture, was demonstrated in a remarkable manner by Louis Kossuth. That illustrious patriot, scholar and statesman, came to our country from the far east of Europe, a complete master of the English language. He spoke our difficult tongue with an eloquence as stately and grand as that of the best American orators. When asked how he obtained this mastery of a language so foreign to him, he told us that his school house was an Austrian prison, and his school books, the Bible, Shakespeare, and an old English dictionary.

Side by side with the great Hungarian, let me name the King of American self-made men; the man who rose highest and will be remembered longest as the most popular and beloved President since Washington—ABRAHAM LINCOLN. This man came to us, not from the schools or from the mansions of ease and luxury, but from the back woods. He mastered his grammar by the light of a pine wood torch. The fortitude and industry which could split rails by day, and learn grammar at night at the hearthstone of a log hut and by the unsteady glare of a pine wood knot, prepared this man for a service to his country and to mankind, which only the most exalted could have performed.

The examples thus far given, belong to the Caucassian race; but to the African race, as well, we are indebted for examples equally worthy and inspiring. Benjamin Bannecker, a man of African descent, born and reared in the state of Maryland, and a contemporary with the great men of the revolution, is worthy to be mentioned with the highest of his class. He was a slave, withheld from all those inspiring motives which freedom, honor and distinction furnish to exertion; and yet this man secured an English education; became a learned mathematician, was an excellent surveyor, assisted to lay out the city of Washington, and compelled honorable recognition from some of the most distinguished scholars and statesmen of that early day of the Republic.

The intellect of the Negro was then, as now, the subject of learned inquiry. Mr. Jefferson, among other statesmen and philosophers, while he considered slavery an evil, entertained a rather low estimate of the Negro's mental ability. He thought that the Negro might become learned in music and in language, but that mathematics were quite out of the question with him.

In this debate Benjamin Bannecker came upon the scene and materially assisted in lifting his race to a higher consideration than that in which it had been previously held. Bannecker was not only proficient as a writer, but, like Jefferson, he was a philosopher. Hearing of Mr. Jefferson's opinion of Negro intellect, he took no offense but calmly addressed that statesman a letter and a copy of an almanac for which he had made the astronomical calculations. The reply of Mr. Jefferson is the highest praise I wish to bestow upon this black self-made man. It is brief and I take great pleasure in presenting it.

PHILADELPHIA, August 30, 1790

SIR:

I thank you sincerely for your letter and the almanac it contains. Nobody more than I do, wishes to see such proofs as you exhibit, that nature has given our black brethren talents equal to those of other colors of men, and that the appearance of the want of them, is owing mainly to the degrading conditions of their existence in Africa and America. I have taken the liberty of sending your almanac to Monsieur Cordozett, Secretary of the Academy of Science at Paris, and a member of the Philanthropic Society, because I considered it a document of which your whole race had a right, for their justification against the doubts entertained of them.

> I am, with great esteem, sir,
> Your most obedient servant,
> THOMAS JEFFERSON

This was the impression made by an intelligent Negro upon the father of American Democracy, in the earlier and better years of the Republic. I wish that it were possible to make a similar impression upon the children of the American Democracy of this generation. Jefferson was not ashamed to call the black man his brother and to address him as a gentleman.

I am sorry that Bannecker was not entirely black, because in the United States, the slightest infusion of Teutonic blood is thought to be sufficient to account for any considerable degree of intelligence found under any possible color of the skin.

But Bannecker is not the only colored example that I can give. While I turn with honest pride to Bannecker, who lived a hundred years ago, and invoke his aid to roll back the tide of disparagement and contempt which pride and prejudice have poured out against the colored race, I can also cite examples of like energy in our own day.

William Dietz, a black man of Albany, New York, with whom I was personally acquainted and of whom I can speak from actual knowledge, is one such. This man by industry, fidelity and general aptitude for business affairs, rose from the humble calling of house servant in the Dudley family of that city, to become the sole manager of the family estate valued at three millions of dollars.

It is customary to assert that the Negro never invented anything, and that, if he were today struck out of life, there would, in twenty years, be nothing left to tell of his existence. Well, this black man; for he was positively and perfectly black; not partially, but WHOLLY black; a man whom, a few years ago, some of our learned ethnologists would have read out of the human family and whom a certain Chief Justice would have turned out of court as a creature having no rights which white men are bound to respect, was one of the very best draftsmen and designers in the state of New York. Mr. Dietz was not only an architect, but he was also an inventor. In this he was a direct contradiction to the maligners of his race. The noble railroad bridge now spanning the Hudson river at Albany, was, in all essential features, designed by William Dietz. The main objection against a bridge across that highway of commerce had been that of its interference with navigation. Of all the designs presented, that of Dietz was the least objectionable on that score, and was, in its essential features, accepted. Mr. Dietz also devised a plan for an elevated railway to be built in Broadway, New York. The great objection to a railway in that famous thoroughfare was then, as now, that of the noise, dust, smoke, obstruction and danger to life and limb, thereby involved. Dietz undertook to remove all these objections by suggesting an elevated railway, the plan of which was, at the time, published in the *Scientific American* and highly commended by the editor of that journal. The then readers of the *Scientific American* read this account of the inventions of William Dietz, but did not know, as I did, that Mr. Dietz was a black man. There was certainly nothing in his name or in his works to suggest the American idea of color.

Among my dark examples I can name no man with more satisfaction than I can Toussaint L'Overture, the hero of Santo Domingo. Though born a slave and held a slave till he was fifty years of age; though, like Bannecker, he was black and showed no trace of Caucassian admixture, history hands him down to us as a brave and generous soldier, a wise and powerful statesmen, an ardent patriot and a successful liberator of his people and of his country.

The cotemporaries of this Haitien chief paint him as without a single moral blemish; while friends and foes alike, accord him the highest ability. In his eulogists no modern hero has been more fortunate than Toussaint L'Overture. History, poetry and eloquence have vied with each other to do him reverence. Wordsworth and Whittier have, in characteristic verse, encircled his brow with a halo of fadeless glory, while Phillips has borne him among the gods in something like Elijah's chariot of fire.

The testimony of these and a thousand others who have come up from depths of society, confirms the theory that industry is the most potent factor in the success of self-made men, and thus raises the dignity of labor; for whatever may be one's natural gifts, success, as I have said, is due mainly to this great means, open and free to all.

A word now upon the third point suggested at the beginning of this paper; namely, the friendly relation and influence of American ideas and institutions to this class of men.

America is said, and not without reason, to be preeminently the home and patron of self-made men. Here, all doors fly open to them. They may aspire to any position. Courts, Senates and Cabinets, spread rich carpets for their feet, and they stand among our foremost men in every honorable service. Many causes have made it easy, here, for this class to rise and flourish, and first among these causes is the general respectability of labor. Search where you will, there is no country on the globe where labor is so respected and the laborer so honored, as in this country. The conditions in which American society originated; the free spirit which framed its independence and created its government based upon the will of the people, exalted both labor and laborer. The strife between capital and labor is, here, comparatively equal. The one is not the haughty and powerful master and the other the weak and abject slave as is the case in some parts of Europe. Here, the man of toil is not bowed, but erect and strong. He feels that capital is not more indispensable than labor, and he can therefore meet the capitalist as the representative of an equal power.

Of course these remarks are not intended to apply to the states where slavery has but recently existed. That system was the extreme degradation of labor, and though happily now abolished its consequences still linger and may not disappear for a century. To-day, in the presence of the capitalist, the Southern black laborer stands abashed, confused and intimidated. He is compelled to beg his fellow worm to give him leave to toil. Labor can never be respected where the laborer is despised. This is today, the great trouble at the South. The land owners still resent emancipation and oppose the elevation of labor. They have yet to learn that a condition of affairs well suited to a time of slavery may not be well suited to a time of freedom. They will one day learn that large farms and ignorant laborers are as little suited to the South as to the North.

But the respectability of labor is not, as already intimated, the only or the most powerful cause of the facility with which men rise from humble conditions to affluence and importance in the United States. A more subtle and powerful influence is exerted by the fact that the principle of measuring and valuing men according to their respective merits and without regard to their antecedents, is better established and more generally enforced here than in any other country. In Europe, greatness is often thrust upon men. They are made legislators by birth.

> "A king can make a belted knight,
> A marquis, duke and a' that."

But here, wealth and greatness are forced by no such capricious and arbitrary power. Equality of rights brings equality of positions and dignities. Here society very properly saves itself the trouble of looking up a man's kinsfolks in order to determine his grade in life and the measure of respect due him. It cares very little who was his father or grandfather. The boast of the Jews, "We have Abraham for our father," has no practical significance here. He who demands consideration on the strength of a reputation of a dead father, is, properly enough, rewarded with derision. We have no reverence to throw away in this wise.

As a people, we have only a decent respect for our seniors. We cannot be beguiled into accepting empty-headed sons for full-headed fathers. As some one has said, we dispense with the smoke when the candle is out. In popular phrase we exhort every man as he comes upon the stage of active life, "Now do your level best!" "Help yourself!" "Put your shoulder to the wheel!" "Make your own record!" "Paddle your own canoe!" "Be the architect of your own fortune!"

The sons of illustrious men are put upon trial like the sons of common people. They must prove themselves real CLAYS, WEBSTERS and LINCOLNS, if they would attract to themselves the cordial respect and admiration generally awarded to their brilliant fathers. There is, here, no law of entail or primogeniture.

Our great men drop out from their various groups and circles of greatness as bright meteors vanish from the blue overhanging sky bearing away their own silvery light and leaving the places where they once shone so brightly, robed in darkness till relighted in turn by the glory of succeeding ones.

I would not assume that we are entirely devoid of affection for families and for great names. We have this feeling, but it is a feeling qualified and limited by the popular thought; a thought which springs from the heart of free institutions and is destined to grow stronger the longer these institutions shall endure. George Washington, Jr., or Andrew Jackson, Jr., stand no better chance of being future Presidents than do the sons of Smith or Jones, or the sons of anybody else.

We are in this, as Edmund Quincy once said of the rapping spirits, willing to have done with people when they are done with us. We reject living pretenders if they come only in the old clothes of the dead.

We have as a people no past and very little present, but a boundless and glorious future. With us, it is not so much what has been, or what is now, but what is to be in the good time coming. Our mottoes are "Look ahead!" and "Go ahead!", and especially the latter. Our moral atmosphere is full of the inspiration of hope and courage. Every man has his chance. If he cannot be President he can, at least, be prosperous. In this respect, America is not only the exception to the general rule, but the social wonder of the world. Europe, with her divine-right governments and ultra-montane doctrines; with her sharply defined and firmly fixed classes; each class content if it can hold its own against the others, inspires little of individual hope or courage. Men, on all sides, endeavor to continue from youth to old age in their several callings and to abide in their several stations. They seldom hope for anything more or better than this. Once in a while, it is true, men of extraordinary energy and industry, like the Honorable John Bright and the Honorable Lord Brougham, (men whose capacity and disposition for work always left their associates little or nothing to do) rise even in England. Such men would rise to distinction anywhere. They do not disprove the general rule, but confirm it.

What is, in this respect, difficult and uncommon in the Old World, is quite easy and common in the New. To the people of Europe, this eager, ever moving mass which we call American society and in which life is not only a race, but a battle, and everybody trying to get just a little ahead of everybody else, looks very much like anarchy.

The remark is often made abroad that there is no repose in America. We are said to be like the troubled sea, and in some sense this is true. If it is a fact it is also one not without its compensation. If we resemble the sea in its troubles, we also resemble the sea in its power and grandeur, and in the equalities of its particles.

It is said, that in the course of centuries, I dare not say how many, all the oceans of this great globe go through the purifying process of filtration. All their parts are at work and their relations are ever changing. They are, in obedience to ever varying atmospheric forces, lifted from their lowly condition and are borne away by gentle winds or furious storms to far off islands, capes and continents; visiting in their course, mountain, valley and plain; thus fulfilling a beneficent mission and leaving the grateful earth refreshed, enriched, invigorated, beautiful and blooming. Each pearly drop has its fair chance to rise and contribute its share to the health and happiness of the world.

Such, in some sort, is a true picture of the restless activity and ever-changing relations of American society. Like the sea, we are constantly rising above, and returning to, the common level. A small son follows a great father, and a poor son, a rich father. To my mind we have no reason to fear that either wealth, knowledge or power will here be monopolized by the few as against the many.

These causes which make America the home and foster-mother of self-made men, combined with universal suffrage, will, I hope, preserve us from this danger. With equal suffrage in our hands, we are beyond the power of families, nationalities or races.

Then, too, our national genius welcomes humanity from every quarter and grants to all an equal chance in the race of life.

> "We ask not for his lineage,
> We ask not for his name;
> If manliness be in his heart,
> He noble birth may claim.
> We ask not from what land he came,
> Nor where his youth was nursed;
> If pure the stream, it matters not
> The spot from whence it burst."

Under the shadow of a great name, Louis Napoleon could strike down the liberties of France and erect the throne of a despot; but among a people so jealous of liberty as to revolt at the idea of electing, for a third term, one of our best Presidents, no such experiment as Napoleon's could ever be attempted here.

We are sometimes dazzled by the gilded show of aristocratic and monarchical institutions, and run wild to see a prince. We are willing that the nations which enjoy these superstitions and follies shall enjoy them in peace. But, for ourselves, we want none of them and will have none of them and can have none of them while the spirit of liberty and equality animates the Republic.

A word in conclusion, as to the criticisms and embarrassments to which self-made men are exposed, even in this highly favored country. A traveler through the monarchies of Europe is annoyed at every turn by a demand for his passport. Our government has imposed no such burden, either upon the traveler or upon itself. But citizens and private individuals, in their relation to each other and the world, demand of every one the equivalent of a passport to recognition, in the possession of some quality or acquirement which shall commend its possessor to favor. We believe in making ourselves pretty well acquainted with the character, business and history of all comers. We say to all such, "Stand and deliver!" And to this demand self-made men are especially subject.

There is a small class of very small men who turn their backs upon any one who presumes to be anybody, independent of Harvard, Yale, Princeton or other similar institutions of learning. These individuals cannot believe that any good can come out of Nazareth. With them, the diploma is more than the man. To that moral energy upon which depends the lifting of humanity, which is the world's true advancement, these are utter strangers. To them the world is never indebted for progress, and they may safely be left to the gentle oblivion which will surely overtake them.

By these remarks, however, there is meant no disparagement of learning. With all my admiration for self-made men, I am far from considering them the best made men. Their symmetry is often marred by the effects of their extra exertion. The hot rays of the sun and the long and rugged road over which they have been compelled to travel, have left their marks, sometimes quite visibly and unpleasantly, upon them.

While the world values skill and power, it values beauty and polish, as well. It was not alone the hard good sense and honest heart of Horace Greely, the self-made man, that made the *New York Tribune;* but likewise the brilliant and thoroughly educated men silently associated with him.

There never was a self-educated man, however well-educated, who, with the same exertion, would not have been better educated by the aid of schools and colleges. The charge is made and well sustained, that self-made men are not generally over modest or self-forgetful men. It was said of Horace Greeley, that he was a self-made man and worshipped his maker. Perhaps the strong resistance which such men meet in maintaining their claim, may account for much of their self-assertion.

The country knows by heart, and from his own lips, the story of Andrew Jackson. In many cases, the very energies employed, the obstacles overcome, the heights attained and the broad contrasts at every step forced upon the attention, tend to incite and strengthen egotism. A man indebted for himself to himself, may naturally think well of himself.

But this is apt to be far overdone. That a man has been able to make his own way in the world, is an humble fact as well as an honorable one. It is, however, possible to state a very humble fact in a very haughty manner, and self-made men are, as a class, much addicted to this habit. By this peculiarity they make themselves much less agreeable to society than they would otherwise be.

One other criticism upon these men is often very properly made. Having never enjoyed the benefits of schools, colleges and other like institutions of learning, they display for them a contempt which is quite ridiculous and which also makes them appear so. A man may know much about educating himself, and but little about the proper means for educating others. A self-made man is also liable to be full of contrarieties. He may be large, but at the same time, awkward; swift, but ungraceful; a man of power, but deficient in the polish and amiable proportions of the affluent and regularly educated man. I think that, generally, self-made men answer more or less closely to this description.

For practical benefit we are often about as much indebted to our enemies, as to our friends; as much to the men who hiss, as to those who applaud; for it may be with men as some one has said about tea; that if you wish to get its strength, you must put it into hot water. Criticism took Theodore Parker from a village pulpit and gave him the whole country for a platform and the whole nation for an audience. England laughed at American authorship and we sent her Emerson and Uncle Tom's Cabin. From its destitution of trees, Scotland was once a by-word; now it is a garden of beauty. Five generations ago, Britain was ashamed to write books in her own tongue. Now her language is spoken in all quarters of the globe. The Jim Crow Minstrels have, in many cases, led the Negro to the study of music; while the doubt cast upon the Negro's tongue has sent him to the lexicon and grammar and to the study of Greek orators and orations.

Thus detraction paves the way for the very perfections which it doubts and denies.

Ladies and gentlemen: Accept my thanks for your patient attention. I will detain you no longer. If, by statement, argument, sentiment or example, I have awakened in any, a sense of the dignity of labor or the value of manhood, or have stirred in any mind, a courageous resolution to make one more effort towards self-improvement and higher usefulness, I have not spoken altogether in vain, and your patience is justified.